Passive Income

Work From Home and Generate Passive Income

(Start Earning Smart Passive Income With No Capital Required)

David Sandstrom

Published By **Jackson Denver**

David Sandstrom

Passive Income: Work From Home and Generate Passive Income (Start Earning Smart Passive Income With No Capital Required)

ISBN   978-1-998927-25-8

No part of this guidebook shall be reproduced in any form without permission in writing from the publisher except in the case of brief quotations embodied in critical articles or reviews.

Legal & Disclaimer

The information contained in this book is not designed to replace or take the place of any form of medicine or professional medical advice. The information in this book has been provided for educational & entertainment purposes only.

The information contained in this book has been compiled from sources deemed reliable, and it is accurate to the best of the Author's knowledge; however, the Author cannot guarantee its accuracy and validity and cannot be held liable for any errors or omissions. Changes are periodically made to this book. You must consult your doctor or get professional medical advice before using any of the suggested remedies, techniques, or information in this book.

Table Of Contents

Chapter 1: 40 Mind For Passive Income

1. Purchase and rent real property (e.G. Rental, residence, commercial enterprise premises). Your earnings are the difference a number of the loan installment and the lease gathered from tenants, or the entire rent if you acquire the assets together together with your non-public coins.

2. Rent a assets for a coworking workplace – you want employees to allow clients in, rate them, and to do cleaning.

3. Rent an condominium and sublet rooms with the consent of the owner. You can maximize your income with the useful resource of developing the usual of the apartment, equipping the rooms with new furniture, growing more prices, or with the aid of the use of protection together with repainting, transferring a kitchen to a corridor and converting it with an extra room, or maintaining apart one or more

greater rooms if the arrangement of home home windows allows it. These strategies want to come up with an opportunity to fee tenants more than you pay to the owner.

4. Purchase an condominium in a resort in a location with huge touristic traffic, and cooperate with a organisation that enables quick-term leases for tourists. The company gives with acquiring bookings, visitor services, and washing and cleansing. You need to earn as plenty as 30% of the apartment earnings.

5. Sublet part of your apartment inside the short or long time if you have an available lockable room in the condominium, or rent it to site visitors on Airbnb.

6. Create a small warehouse inside the unfastened space of your condo – many personal humans or small businesses need an area to shop their matters.

7. Group funding – in case you can not financially discover the coins for actual

belongings and do no longer need to take out a loan, you could make investments with other human beings. The same applies to solar farms, power-producing windmills, buying centers, enjoyment parks, startups, and many others. Look for such businesses or for agencies that offer precise investment opportunities for clients.

eight. Purchase and lease land – you earn at the distinction some of the mortgage installment and the hire collected from tenants. Lands for hire are regularly looked for thru solar energy organizations, cellular network operators, and automobile parking space investors.

9. Purchase and divide land into smaller plots than may be rented as allotment gardens.

10. Purchase land, construct garages, and hire the garages.

11. Purchase land, gather warehouses, and hire the gap.

12. Purchase land, and bring together a parking lot – you could automate it with a parking meter.

13. Erect billboards – if you do no longer personal land on which you may location a billboard, it's miles enough to locate appropriate land, take delivery of as genuine with the landowners that you can area commercials there, and proportion the profits with them.

14. Network advertising and marketing (i.E. Multi-degree advertising and marketing and advertising and marketing) – organising this type of organisation or attaining the extent in which your form operates for your commissions.

15. Franchise your agency – earn at the license price and a percentage of the month-to-month profits, and gain from an obligation for the franchisee to deliver your merchandise. Passive income is normally earned as a franchisor, no longer a

franchisee. Although, there are exceptions, and a franchisor can teach a franchisee the manner to earn passively.

16. Copyrights – books, CDs and DVDs with exercise workouts, tune, video video games, images, software, or images. You create this type of product as soon as, and earn passively on each sale.

17. Rentals – cars, motorhomes, boats, light aircraft, advertising trailers, garages, computers, warehouses, image machine, song device, vacuums, or washers. You should buy anything that may be rented and get maintain of a everyday passive income.

18. Lend money – gather monthly payments plus your passive profits.

19. Self-provider machine – vending machines with food and drinks, slot machines, self-issuer gasoline stations, laundries, or computerized car washes.

20. Licenses – much like a franchise, but you have not any manipulate over the financial ordinary usual performance of the licensee. You most effective promote your understanding.

21. Invest – you lend cash to someone who wishes to shop for cheap flats, renovate them, and promote them for a earnings. You percent the profits.

22. Leasing investment – leasing machines, gadgets, or vehicles. You can rent a automobile and lease it for extra than the lease.

23. Patent rights – rights granted to an inventor. If a person else wants to use your art work, you can earn passively on it. There are folks that regularly patent their thoughts.

24. An island in a shopping center – one salesclerk is enough for automation.

25. Automated organisation – any business organization that can be positioned below the responsibility of others (e.G. Commercial enterprise accomplice, worker). It is difficult to automate commercial organization this is based in your one-of-a-kind abilities, collectively with photographs painted on your specific fashion that most effective you could make to reserve.

26. Positioned internet website online / blog / vlog with your products – you publish a piece of writing as quickly as, it really is your art work, and then promote your products whilst all of us engages together in conjunction with your content material.

27. Paid get entry to to your know-how – this can be private social media groups, or paid content to your internet internet website online.

28. Earnings from advertising on a weblog, for your films on YouTube, and many others.

29. Affiliate packages – in case you need a product, you can advocate it to others. Preferably in an automatic way, which includes on a landing internet web page.

30. Create records-products together with on-line publications, e-books, audiobooks, e mail courses, device lists, paid webinars, publications, checklists, workbooks with carrying sports, planners, movies, recordings of interviews with professionals, infographics, calendars, audio courses, and so forth.

31. Subscriptions – a reoccurring charge to be used of your autoresponder, plug-in, invoicing software software, touchdown net net web page application, snap shots software program, picture net web page, utility, and so forth.

32. Automated distribution (i.E. Brokerage) – paid commercials that robotically appear on categorized net web sites, reserving internet sites that rate a price for every

booking, net websites that offer employer statistics for a charge, product assessment web sites, on-line bookstores, and so forth.

33. Application – commercials, links to associate packages, in-app purchases.

34. Selling bodily merchandise to your on-line save or shopping for and promoting systems, and automating the manner with the aid of storing them in transport warehouses with an worker that handles shipping.

35. Financial merchandise – mutual price range, bonds, deposits, financial savings debts, and so on.

36. Purchase of stocks in dividend agencies and receiving dividends.

37. Advertising on your vehicle, fence, or balcony.

38. A month-to-month rate – corporations that reward you month-to-month for bringing a client. For instance, an accounting

workplace that gives you 10% in their profits from the client.

39. Buy a cryptocurrency excavator, specially if you use solar panels and do now not want to pay for the important strength.

forty. Dropshipping – you do not need to worry approximately stock or shipping products. Instead, even as you obtain an order from a consumer, order records is sent to the wholesaler who then sends products right now to the customer.

Chapter 2: How I Created 10 Passive Earning

1. FLAT FOR RENT

1. I labored whole-time as an assistant to the general director of a large business enterprise. I did no longer just like the way, so I changed into stimulated to look for specific opportunities. I loved studying and came in the course of books approximately economic freedom. I become positive this changed into the answer for me. From that second on, I changed into determined to create passive earnings that would allow me to stop my undertaking.

2. I placed that my profits are sufficient to take out a mortgage and purchase an rental to rent.

three. I took gain of this case and searched for the precise condo.

four. I provided an empty forty -square-meter, three-room condo subsequent to a metro station.

Quick calculation: the charge of the apartment grow to be 405,000 PLN. The buy prices (e.G. Tax, notary) totaled 10,000 PLN.

My contribution to the mortgage have become 60,000 PLN. Half of my contribution became a loan from my circle of relatives. They moreover helped me refresh the condominium. I supplied fixtures for 20,000 PLN. The loan installment become 1,900 PLN month-to-month. I lease the condo for two,4 hundred PLN plus administrative rent and utilities consistent with intake.

five. My first passive profits may not were extremely good at 500 PLN month-to-month, from which I paid off the mortgage from my circle of relatives over the following five years, however I knew the condominium coins would possibly in the end pay off my financial group mortgage, and inside the a long manner future, all the rent might be my passive earnings.

2. AUTOMATED COMPANY

1. Apartments rented for days, cheaper than a hotel, frequently greater spacious, with their personal kitchen and rest room seemed to be a first-rate concept for a first agency.

2. I wrote an utility for funding to begin a corporation. One of the requirements was a enormously unique advertising and marketing approach. I did proper studies and knew hundreds approximately this industrial agency.

three. I browsed the gives of houses for lease. Next, I known as one of the proprietors and prepared a assembly to see an apartment and signal a lease settlement.

four. I determined a business associate – my fiancé.

5. I picked up keys to the condo, refreshed it, supplied lodge device (e.G. Bed linens, towels, cosmetics, bathrobes), took photographs, published classified ads online, and purchased the first bookings.

6. I did now not accumulate cash from funding. We invested our private coins. The funding end up 6,000 PLN for the number one month's rent, deposit, condominium refreshment and hotel system.

7. When we had 5 flats and have been wonderful the enterprise may generate an terrific profits, I give up my machine. I had more time, so we duplicated our sports activities until we obtained 20 homes. With every operating apartment, I had extra and extra cash for investment in renting extra houses and for hiring personnel to carry out the paintings.

Quick calculation: the month's hire for a small studio condominium changed into 1,700 PLN. For a one-day reserving, I earned

100 and 80 PLN. If the condo emerge as absolutely booked, I earned 5,four hundred PLN consistent with month. It come to be usually sincerely booked because of its right area, expert ad snap shots, cutting-edge format and pinnacle evaluations.

eight. We computerized the company by using way of writing down all the guidelines of its operation and schooling personnel to work independently. Moreover, we partnered with a pal in order to have more manipulate of the financial enterprise. It took approximately a one year from release of the concept to earn passive earnings.

three. INVESTMENTS

1. I did no longer enjoy stable with most effective one income. I favored to make investments to ordinary and multiply my cash.

2. I examine some books approximately constructing an funding portfolio, looked for answers at the Internet, and most

significantly, I searched for agencies that might assist me pick out out investments that offer passive income often, now not as quickly as.

3. I participated in an thrilling education path given by means of using a commercial enterprise company that chooses the pleasant funding sports to be had in the marketplace that supply passive earning (e.G. Funding in bank power vegetation, joint buy of actual estate, buy of stocks with dividend), and installation cooperation with it.

four. I selected gives from this organization that interested me the maximum and transferred cash for the first funding. When it turned out that everything have end up outstanding, and I need to see that it actually works, I decided on the following investments.

5. It took 365 days from release of the concept to earn passive income. Usually, my

earnings is paid as soon as a 12 months. The fee of go back on those investments have become commonly approximately 10%.

4. FRANCHISE

1. During a private improvement education, I met a person at some stage in networking who heard what I do, and requested me for help in putting in a company like mine in some different metropolis. I concluded that it changed into a notable idea, and I must help.

2. I created a license settlement.

4. We signed a agreement and started to cooperate.

5. I visited the metropolis and did marketplace studies, supplied all files on which I wrote down the technique of operation and automation of my agency business enterprise, helped in renting the primary apartments, equipping them and obtaining the number one bookings. I did

not invest any cash. I charged licensors an initial fee that covered all my fees, which incorporates fuel and lodging. Generally, I exceeded on virtually acceptable expertise, and after months I earned my first passive earnings from my first franchise. I now earn it month-to-month.

6. I created a easy blog approximately renting homes brief-term. I paid 1,000 PLN to create it.

7. I wrote weblog posts that percentage my facts, and independently positioned them with the beneficial aid of using appropriate key terms and through way of using a smooth WordPress plugin. I placed a franchising offer under the posts. It turned into easy to discover my offer at the Internet, manner to which greater human beings favored to cooperate with me.

9. I duplicated my sports activities up to fifteen licenses everywhere within the america (one regular with every huge city

that has business and vacationer site visitors). I earn passively.

5. AFFILIATE PROGRAMS

1. I had been seeking out every other passive income and wanted to use my weblog.

2. For one of the articles on my weblog, I interviewed a person who earned cash on affiliate packages. I grow to be interested by it, and after this interview, had some records about how to do it.

3. I searched for thoughts for associate applications at the Internet. I selected products and services that I was inquisitive about and which have been related to the problem of my blog.

4. I commenced out to cooperate with a few businesses in the fields of economic freedom and personal development trainings, selling books, tour booking, and financial investments.

5. I wrote articles and included records approximately the gives.

For instance – I wrote a put up approximately books that helped me in my private development, and connected every identify to my accomplice companion net web site that sells the e-book. When a person who check my article sold a e-book I recommended, I earned a percent of the purchase quantity. I did the same for locations I booked for the duration of journey. People who examine approximately my travels had an opportunity to pick out the identical area and e-book it, and I earned a fee from it.

I did not make investments any cash. It changed into very clean to hyperlink to my partners, and I did it on my own.

7. I get maintain of a part of the earnings from earnings passively as it works routinely on my net internet site. About three months

handed from launch of the concept earlier than I earned passive profits.

6. ONLINE COURSE

1. I actually have end up already financially unfastened, had know-how observed by enterprise employer achievement, and preferred to share my enjoy with the resource of developing a web path.

2. I took element in an online course approximately sharing facts as an expert. Its educate defined precisely the manner to create my private product on-line.

three. The route lasted 5 weeks, and I did exactly the whole thing the educate stated: I created video substances, a proposal, and deliberate the platform for the route.

4. I decided a person who created a course platform for me, and paid 2,000 PLN for it.

5. As you apprehend, I located every of my blog articles with determined on key phrases. Additionally, I had been frequently

commenting on unique blogs to have a better function in on line seek effects. I used terms together with "passive profits" or "monetary freedom". In this manner, I prevented paid marketing and positioned it totally unfastened and naturally – all and sundry who looked for records about passive earnings online came to my blog and observed a product (i.E. My online path) ideally fitted to their goals.

6. I earn passively. About four months passed from release of the concept earlier than I earned passive profits.

7. RENTING ROOMS LONG-TERM

1. I already knew the way to make coins through renting an condominium with out being its proprietor. I had an idea that in addition to a brief-term condominium, I might also moreover attempt an extended-time period sublease.

2. I have been seeking out apartments the rate of to be able to be with out issues

extended thru quick refreshment or thru being divided into rooms.

three. I were regularly looking the apartments.

five. I located three suitable apartments and rented them for the longest viable duration.

7. I discovered a renovation crew, they refreshed the rental, and allocated extra rooms. We prepared it with new furnishings. Quick calculation for one rental: one month's rent turn out to be three,000 PLN, deposit turn out to be 3,000 PLN, and safety with new fixtures and tool grow to be eight,000 PLN. The flats have been 85 square meters, had 3 rooms, however after maintenance, five rooms. Every room became 12 square meters. I rent every room for 1,000 PLN to more youthful human beings. I earn 2,000 PLN consistent with month. My funding can pay for itself after seven months. There is a sensible rule in this commercial agency – the funding in an

condo ought to pay off within three hundred and sixty 5 days.

eight. I had a photo consultation and posted offers on labeled web web sites.

nine. I rented rooms to tenants. One room - one character.

10. I favored to art work quicker. I provided a software program to find out appropriate housing gives from numerous assets. I paid 800 PLN in step with twelve months.

11. I duplicated my sports activities with the resource of renting extra residences. Now, I without a doubt have twelve. About 3 months surpassed from release of the idea before I earned passive earnings from the primary rooms.

eight. BOOK

1. I truly have commonly wanted to put in writing a ebook. By hazard, I observed an business about an interesting on-line direction. Its creators promised to educate

the way to write and placed up a book in three months.

2. I took up the mission and did the whole lot the instructors taught. In the technique of writing, I had a pre-sale, which instructed me how many quantities I need to area up on the begin. Moreover, I did now not make investments my very very very own money inside the e-book.

three. I located contractors to do proofreading, enhancing, cover layout and printing.

4. I took the posted books to a shipping warehouse.

five. I enclosed a suggestion to buy a ebook on my net website, did a campaign on Facebook, and participated in several public appearances to reveal my ebook.

6. I began to cooperate with six wholesalers that address e book distribution. I sent them

books. My ebook now seems in almost each online e-book region.

7. I earn passively promoting the e-book on my weblog and to wholesalers. It took approximately six months from release of the idea to regular passive profits, but I generated the number one income all through the pre-sale after approximately one month.

Quick calculation: one 250-internet page e-book price approximately 10 PLN to print. I promote one e book for 40 PLN, with domestic delivery for 10 PLN included. I earn 20 PLN for one ebook.

Earnings are a hint decrease with wholesalers.

nine. CRYPTOCURRENCY MINING STATION

1. I wrote an software for investment for my associate to begin a agency, with the justification that he desired a higher laptop with awesome images playing playing cards

in an effort to create expert pix for his future customers. We obtained 20,000 PLN for this reason.

2. We sold a motherboard, processor, lovers and their controls, photographs playing gambling cards, risers and power belongings.

three. We located it all together with an IT colleague and set it as a lot as mine Ethereum. It took severa days to check its abilities and find the satisfactory mining parameters, and to set up wallets in which we ought to store mined cryptocurrencies.

four. Quick calculation: our mining station earns on commonplace 40 PLN every 24 hours, which equals approximately 1, hundred PLN month-to-month. Deducting the month-to-month fee of electricity, the passive income is 900 PLN.

10. ONLINE SHOP

1. For more than one years I were interested in spiritual improvement and ecological lifestyles, so I started to create physical products related to the ones situation subjects to promote in an internet maintain.

2. I located a company companion.

3. My commercial organisation companion knew someone who may also want to create jewelry. We gave this person our designs and he created the primary merchandise prepared to sell.

3. We ordered creation of an internet store, took pix, wrote descriptions of the goods, and started to write down posts for our new blog and social media.

four. When we began out receiving orders, we focused on developing exceptional products, and on writing posts to boom sales.

five. We created some merchandise ourselves (e.G. Gratitude mag, relaxation playing gambling cards) and took others from wholesalers (e.G. Chrome steel bottles, yoga mats).

6. We employed an employee to deal with delivery.

7. We earn passively but work on new products if there may be a want. We like this industrial corporation, however it's miles proper to have a desire to artwork or not. If you love your technique, you can not art work for a minute.

Below, you can observe a number of my subjective conclusions on being financially loose. I additionally solution the maximum not unusual questions I certainly have acquired in ultra-modern years.

Firstly, it wasn't continuously smooth. I even have written out in factors the manner to generate a passive earnings, just so it might be a good deal much less difficult so as to repeat these specific steps.

However, I did now not cross into detail about a number of the failures, in reality one in each of which changed into losing earning – an automated business enterprise and its franchise for the duration of the coronavirus pandemic. I am conscious that I can lose everything in life, however manner to the massive diversification of my earnings, I got here out of it unscathed.

I even have generated such a variety of wonderful incomes due to the truth I like to check one-of-a-type answers and need to expose my weblog readers many opportunities. You do now not want to have 10 passive earning to be financially free. Once I heard very sensible terms from my educate: "It won't rely how many businesses you have got, how heaps cash is positioned to your debts, how big of an income you acquire, or what you have were given built, because you could lose the whole thing. Your records is the most essential, due to the fact with information and experience you can with out problem rebuild it at any time and location. Don't worry if some thing is going wrong or you lose a few problem alongside the way. Nobody is going to take what you've got discovered out."

How do I address it all of sudden and in which did I discover the braveness and motivation to act?

One via way of one – I do not must deal with it all of sudden because of the reality I do one detail at a time.

One trouble at a time. Choose one profits, use my steps, or create your private plan. Next, interest on its first issue.

I simplest start to create every other organization once I accumulate passive income from the previous one.

It is deferred investment due to the truth you need to first make investments some time or cash. This method requires masses of sacrifice and creates a sense of loss of self assurance. Why? Because you do not apprehend if it'll paintings and bring passive earnings.

In my case, seeking out other sports activities modified into genuinely an break out from the problems that I encountered every day. It might be fine if you deliver interest to at least one assignment, awareness on one asset first, convey it to the factor wherein it will supply coins, and then begin the subsequent organisation or funding. Perseverance and attention undergo in thoughts right here.

As for braveness – the entire gadget of getting passive cash can be an awful lot much less difficult for you and it will not scare and discourage you in case you divide it into levels. Believe me, I should in no manner have walked the entire path at some stage in hiking camp if it had now not been divided into 5- to 6-kilometer tiers. Thinking about the complete route, it truly seemed now not viable to cover. When you have a look at taken into consideration one among my steps, does it absolutely seem difficult to conform with? This is one easy mission to check off.

Regarding motivation, I had motivating factors. First of all, I felt uncomfortable in each whole-time hobby, as despite the fact that I changed into trapped in a cage. Secondly, I like to adventure, and passive earnings makes excursion feasible for me. I take delivery of as true with that earning passive profits is feasible for all people determined to become financially impartial.

How did it seem that I performed monetary freedom in most effective more than one years?

I handled economic freedom as a aim, no longer a dream. Wealth and abundance are the natural kingdom of our being. We can't dream of some issue herbal this is accessible. This cause is like a few different reason, collectively with jogging a marathon.

Secondly, I did now not have well-known excuses, which includes loss of cash or time, and at the equal time have become strongly determined to gain my goal.

If you accept as true with you studied that you need masses of coins to create passive earnings, please give up the excuse. Some of my tasks did not require coins the least bit, on the identical time as a few required small amounts of coins to begin. Choose the ones dreams for that you want to spend a while, and get the art work finished, not individuals who require a whole lot of cash. Choose the assets normal at the side of your possibilities and monetary situation.

You in all likelihood can't have sufficient cash to reveal your lifestyles the incorrect manner up and abandon your every day duties to pay attention on your purpose as masses as possible. I turned into in the equal scenario. I started with the purpose that each day after art work I write an software program for funding to begin a enterprise enterprise, which end up moreover a advertising and marketing strategy. I started out out with the aid of creating better use of my loose time. Next, I dedicated all my free time to broadening monetary intelligence with the resource of reading books, searching the Internet, and taking aspect in trainings. Remember, even the smallest victories encourage you to maintain going for walks and make you need to keep conducting your goals.

Chapter 3: Preparing Your Plan

You want to be financially loose, however what does that advocate for you? How a fantastic deal money need to be earned every month?

The bigger your goals, the extra your passive profits must be.

Therefore, please calculate the month-to-month fee of your life-style. It is important to recognize how big the drift of passive income have to be to make you a financially unfastened individual.

To do that, in fact write down all your monthly fees (e.G. Loan installment, gasoline and public shipping, electricity, lease, grocery shopping for, cultural existence, clothes).

Next, list abnormal expenses (e.G. Taking location tour, tire exchange, items for birthdays and vacations, vehicle coverage insurance, scientific appointments, condo renovations, belongings you plan to shop for) and divide them through twelve.

Sum up the everyday and abnormal month-to-month charges and write down the amount.

At the begin of this ebook I asked you to pick out belongings that to begin with interest you, seem maximum suitable for you, and are closest for your passion and skills. If your monetary state of affairs does not permit you to make investments money, you could pick out out assets that can be created alongside aspect your paintings and time, not cash.

Please write down some thoughts for passive profits that you preferred the most.

To be financially loose I want to earn .... passive income month-to-month.

To acquire this, I certainly have determined to create or collect the subsequent property that generate passive income:

1. …………

2. …………

three. …………

four. …………

5. …………

Concentrate on one asset from that you need to begin and write it like this:

The first deliver of passive income that I want to create or acquire is …………

My cut-off date is: ………… date.

For example, your announcement may appear like this:

The first deliver of passive earnings that I will create/acquire is an e-book about my passion on the way to be provided on Amazon.

My cut-off date is 31 July 2022.

Steps I will take to acquire my aim:

1.Write an e-book on a topic that I recognise well and in which I is probably an professional.

2.Watch severa movies on YouTube approximately developing e-books on Amazon.

three.Read numerous articles on the internet approximately promoting e-books on Amazon.

4.If essential, buy the "My first product on Amazon" course.

five.Translate the content material cloth material from Polish to English.

6.Find someone to edit my English model.

7.Use what I discover ways to create the quilt, or discover a person to layout it for me.

eight.Use what I discover ways to create an offer, enter all records, and position the e-book at the platform.

9.Start selling.

10. Check interest within the product and, if important, beautify it as required through patron goals.

In the surrender, specify the time and area in which you may paintings in your plan each day.

As you observe, step one you can take is obtaining information about the selected asset. If you have not any concept approximately some difficulty, you can not see any outcomes and also you gained't have manage over income from that supply. Therefore, listing techniques wherein you can gain the know-how you want, each without value and for rate, in line with your contemporary competencies.

It is ordinary that your plan will no longer be ideal or unique, as you do not have the statistics about the chosen asset however. Write some number one points and begin gaining knowledge. While gaining knowledge of, upload particular obligations to accomplish. You also can upload an predicted crowning glory date to the points (i.E. Milestones) to your way in your cause.

Your plan will alternate with the information to procure. New thoughts and needs will emerge, and that is completely ok. The most vital problem is to behave because of the reality every small step brings you towards economic freedom.

Chapter 4: Teespring

For the creatives reachable or folks that constantly have something witty in thoughts that might be have become in cash, this feature is probably for you. As the decision shows, TeeSpring is a website that allows quite much anybody to layout their very personal shirts and promote it for a profits. All you want to begin developing is to be had thru their system so you can get started out without the need to make investments A LOT of coins surely to get matters rolling. But first, allow's address the necessities.

The Company

TeeSpring is an e-trade platform that allows truely every body from anywhere within the international to with out problems create merchandise and then sell their merchandise on-line. They take customization to a completely new degree, making it extra to be had for all of us. Using the business organisation's "TeeSpring Launcher" clients might be able to pick out the form of item they would really like to sell and pick out out the color they pick out earlier than which includes a layout.

The wonderful bit right here is that designs can actually be uploaded from out of doors the internet site, a feature that works superb for creatives who have their private images prepared for the undertaking. For others who are beginning from scratch, but, they may use severa gear made available at the platform itself. This method is the maximum hands-on a company can get for TeeSpring will address the relaxation from there. They'll take care of manufacturing and distribution, which include patron offerings for any products sold through their internet web site.

Note: All the goods presented on the net website are artificial in numerous facilities across the world.

Say, you're a small designer with large mind looking for a manner to show all that into earnings—TeeSpring is one of the notable avenues to try this.

What Can You Sell on TeeSpring?

You can choose out from a enormous kind of clothing, permitting you to in shape your merchandise with your preferred market.

-Shirts

-Sweatshirts

-Hoodies

-Children's put on

-Leggings

Users can also loose up unique products to embody of their stock, which incorporates:

-Plushies

-Pins

-Hats

-Phone times

How Much Can You Earn on TeeSpring?

First off, TeeSpring may be used for free of charge. You set your very very own pricing for every product you're making and get to keep a hundred% of the profits as properly. To located it clearly:

The base fee for t-shirts on the net internet site is $10. If you choose out out to promote the item for $25, you get to preserve $15 in earnings.

When setting charges, you need to aspect in sure information an amazing manner to have an impact on the lowest charge. Here's what you need to keep in mind:

-The amount of colours you used for your format.

-The amount of objects supplied for each listing.

-If your design has a print on each the the the front and the yet again.

-Discounts. This can be acquired depending on the variety of gadgets you have been able to sell inside the course of the previous month.

Note that product base fees, collectively with bargain degrees, may be visible on the internet site itself. Always are seeking out recommendation from this listing earlier than you finalize your very own product pricing to ensure you're no longer below or overpricing your products.

Getting Started with TeeSpring – Step by way of manner of the use of Step Guide

This is a pretty straightforward way, one that's moreover especially chance-free, depending at the approach you operate for designing your shirts. All you really want is a stable layout idea and you can start selling inner an hour. Here's what you want to do:

- Start thru manner of making an account at the net internet site. They may require your touch information and you'll be made to pick the techniques via which you need to get hold of your commissions. Options encompass: direct deposit, paper cheque, or thru PayPal. Choose the one that's maximum handy for you.

- Before continuing, make sure you undergo the Terms and situations. If you're making plans on using third birthday celebration designers in some unspecified time in the destiny, there are key elements to undergo in mind and do not forget. The vital detail right here is to make sure you're aware of possible copyright troubles—violating these can purpose your maintain getting closed.

- Study up. You'll discover beneficial gaining knowledge of system on the internet site itself, which include an introductory video, a ninety-minute video that need to help you get better familiar with how matters artwork, and a checklist a good way to make certain you've got the whole thing you need. That's about 2 hours of exertions but comprehend that it gained't visit waste. The extra and the better you understand TeeSpring, the better your chances at succeeding.

- Begin designing your shirt. Now, there are some techniques via which you could try this.

•If you have got the abilities and information, you can create your format from scratch and sincerely add it to the website after. Artists can use this to create merch the use of their art work—anyways, now not absolutely all of us desires a print to understand on their partitions. Sometimes, sensible art work is what's marketable.

•What if you don't have the capabilities? Well, this is in which 1/3-party designers are available in on hand. You'll be able to find them via structures which incorporates Craigslist, Fiverr, Freelancer, and Upwork. Note that due to the fact you're hiring an extra hand and could need to pay for the ones services, element that into your pricing. Make certain which you gained't have copyright troubles at the facet of your hired designer as properly!

•Establish your pricing. For this, a chunk of more studies is fundamental. Here are a few tips:

o Shirts sell better in case you stay in the $15 - $25 price variety. This moreover relies upon within the market you're promoting to, however the above is quite much less costly for the not unusual individual.

o Hoodies sell higher if you preserve it within the $30 to $40 nine range.

o First time dealers on TeeSpring typically stay with the ones forms of clothing due to the fact that they'll be the maximum well-known. Once you've installation your emblem and function learned extra approximately your area of interest, then you could recall branching out to different merchandise.

•Think about your earnings goal. Once you've decided how loads your gadgets are going to price, you furthermore mght want to installation a profits reason. This elements to the minimal amount of merchandise you want to sell so as to your shirts to get found out. The range is truely up to you and your options range from 5 as much as a thousand. Keep in mind that the better your variety, the extra cash you'll be making for every sale. NOTE: If you don't gain your minimal intention, your shirts will no longer be posted. This is why you want to find out a niche in your products and make certain the marketplace is willing to resource you.

•Give your advertising advertising campaign or challenge a name. The more charming and thrilling the call, the better it'll be for you. After, set the duration for it—this may variety everywhere from 3 to 21 days. U.S. Based completely orders will start arriving about per week or so after your marketing campaign ends.

•Marketing. Okay, so you need to reach your reason and get your goal market to shop for. This is one way of making that rise up. You can use numerous social media structures for this cause. Good vintage faculty e-mail marketing can also do the trick. This is likewise why an extended advertising campaign duration is beneficial—you'll have greater time to spread the phrase and generate hobby. Again, your shirts will best go to print if the advertising and marketing marketing campaign meets the income purpose. Otherwise, your clients will no longer be charged and you could typically try over again.

What happens if you do meet your earnings aim? If you be successful earlier than the advertising and marketing advertising and marketing campaign ends, your t-shirt format is going into print and is then allocated via TeeSpring to anybody who ordered. All that's left if you need to do is stay up for the profits to are available in.

Tips for Beginners

- Keep a watch constant constant out for dispositions. Capitalize on what every body's speakme about—this includes diverse memes and trending topics. This is splendid in case you don't have a selected community in mind, without a doubt make sure you test up on copyright pointers so you can avoid mishaps.

- Always offer your customers with options. Around three to four color options are commonly specific to have—anyways, every body has excellent tastes.

- Beginners ought to constantly start out with smaller desires, about 10 to twenty need to be sufficient. What if your campaign is ready to end and you're nonetheless a ways from your dreams? Experts recommend which you lower the range.

Doing so will help ensure that to procure some profits for all the effort you placed into it.

- Invest in ADs. You do now not need to spend loads however doing this will not quality make you more acquainted with the technique, it'll additionally assist set up you as a brand.

- Always do your research. Aside from the technical element of factors, you could furthermore want to find out what other designers are doing. Remember that even when you have preceding experience in this industry, there'll normally be room for improvement. There are numerous organizations in Facebook that cater to this unique cause so don't hesitate on the subject of collaborating.

- Know that you can fail the number one few times. Most designers, regardless of the volume of expertise, might possibly find that their first few attempts isn't profitable. This is excellent ordinary and also you shouldn't allow it discourage you from persevering with. The crucial element here is to preserve trying—the greater you do it, the extra you'll get a revel in for what sells and what doesn't. You'll want every enjoy and time if you need to in reality be successful.

- Experiment. Test unique forms of ADs and check which one yields the most earnings. The beginning might be slow, however that's a part of the gaining knowledge of curve. Never rush the manner for doing so might cost you extra money than you'll be able to get lower back.

Keep in thoughts, as with all begin-up, everything will enjoy slow within the beginning. Of path, you need to start earning as quickly as viable—but that's no longer the mind-set you want to have transferring in advance. Otherwise, you'd surrender getting sorely disillusioned because of the fact you're no longer earning as lots as you concept you'll.

Take subjects sluggish, observe as you pass,
and maintain at it.

Chapter 5: Merch By Amazon

One of the maximum well-known approaches of creating passive profits online is via way of selling numerous merchandise—however, will that be viable in case you take place to have zero budget for capital and may simplest depend upon your very very own creativity to get subjects going? The answer is YES. There are techniques to make your employer show up without making an funding a whole lot of coins to get it up and going for walks.

That's the beauty of the internet, you spot. It affords us with lots of possibilities, just so long as you recognize in which to look. And that's what I'm right right right here to help you with; finding the right structures to on the way to permit you to begin incomes.

This time, we have a very famous name at the desk.

The Company

Surely, you've already heard of or might also additionally have even attempted some of Amazon's many extraordinary products and services. However, no longer many are privy to Merch thru Amazon and the manner it may offer profits opportunities to people who are looking for a manner to earn extra cash.

Merch thru Amazon is a POD or "print on name for" platform that lets in pretty a remarkable deal every body to make a income via promoting in my opinion branded merchandise using gadgets from the net web site's non-public product internet internet page. There's no initial investment required; all you need to do is create an account, upload your format, then click on on on positioned up.

We all recognize how supportive fandoms can be almost about their favorites—Merch with the aid of way of Amazon allows you to offer them with legitimate gadgets and in addition red meat up the network that's helping your paintings. Besides, what higher way to promote your logo than to have fans show off their love for it? And with Amazon looking after all the technical statistics, you can rest easy which you are going for walks with a good company.

What Can You Sell on Merch with the aid of Amazon?

Originally, this application have become launched to help app developers monetize their logo thru the usage of promoting merch. During this time, the goods had been constrained to shirts—however, this gadget has due to the fact advanced to consist of different apparel. Interested buyers can now pick out from:

- Standard shirts

- Premium shirts

- Long sleeve shirts

- Hoodies

- Sweatshirts

Note that there are not every different merchandise presently protected of their inventory—so if you're searching for to promote items which incorporates mugs, tote luggage, hats, and so on. You may want to find a incredible platform other than Amazon.

Applying for Merch thru Amazon

Unlike exclusive comparable POD structures, there can be a trap almost approximately signing up for Amazon's utility. There is an software tool you'll want to get authorized for in advance than you may begin earning earnings. Fortunately, this unique step is quite clean and may be finished internal mins.

- Login on your Amazon account. This may be a dealer's account or a purchaser's account. It can also be a modern one that you're developing specifically for the Merch account.

- Once you're in, begin the software. You may be requested to offer the subsequent records:

•Your business corporation contact records

•Your economic institution account and routing numbers

•Your social protection variety / other tax identification amount

- Next, pinnacle off the tax questionnaire. Now, in case you're placed outdoor of the united states the industrial enterprise employer can withhold as an awful lot as 30% of your profits for tax so do check of this in advance than going through with the software program.

- Once you're completed making ready all that's indexed above, it's time to request an invitation. Getting started out requires an invitation and to get one, you'll ought to go to this page: https://merch.Amazon.Com/landing

wherein you'll discover the bright orange button for invitation requests.

- Don't have a business enterprise installation to your Merch account? No problem. You can use your first and remaining call alternatively. Just make sure that the contact statistics you located up is actual and energetic. You'll want most of these so that it will get your invitation request granted.

Completing the Merch Invitation Request Form

There are three separate sections you need to finish in terms of the invitation request. Here's what to expect:

- Industry Type. On the dropdown menu you'll discover some unique options as a manner to choose out from. If you filled out the software the usage of your non-public name in preference in your business organization's, then I propose going with a novelty shirt company. If you used your company enterprise agency call, but, choose small commercial enterprise from the options as an alternative.

- Organization Name. This is in which you'll be moving into your business employer or your private call—all of it's far primarily based upon on what you submitted within the first internet internet web page of your app. Note that every paperwork need to in shape.

- Additional Info. Remember, you're making use of for an invite so make whole use of this vicinity to make your commercial enterprise business enterprise standout from the alternative candidates. Include any relevant information, on the aspect of great POD designs and internet web sites you've got performed inside the beyond.

Keep in mind that any facts you post must generally be honest.

Tips for Getting Accepted into Merch with the useful resource of way of Amazon

If you want to get normal, you'll need to provide Amazon enough data—essentially, be as obvious as feasible to make sure them that you're a legitimate provider. You want no longer have a photograph layout ancient past in case you need on your request to get large, however here are a few stuff you want to bear in mind which includes to your form:

- If you have POD enjoy, make sure you encompass hyperlinks for your preceding designs and the alternative net websites you have got were given got uploaded them to.

- Have a non-public website? Don't overlook to include that as nicely. You get plus elements if you're already selling on different structures and feature a organized marketplace for your merchandise.

- Include a evidence on your plan on advertising and advertising and marketing and selling your merchandise to Amazon's base intention market. It want not be expertly written, but understand that this is supposed to reveal how plenty enjoy you have were given and if you recognize what you're entering into.

- Create about 5 to ten proper designs. You also can embody current ones that you haven't tried to sell however. Include those in your software program software.

- List down any emblems you personal, in addition to licenses to any art work.

PRO TIP: Understand that none of the above is a considered necessary so as that allows you to get ordinary into the Merch software application. However, they may offer you with a bonus and could help make you standout in opposition to special candidates. Considering the amount of people vying for a gap, each little element that could help make your utility greater appealing to reviewers will clearly gain your goal.

QUICK FAQ: Does Amazon attain designs finished for you through a 3rd birthday celebration? The solution is YES. You have the selection of outsourcing your designs in case you're lacking the talents to make your non-public or truely want some thing distinctive than what you could typically create. Note which you want to steady the copyright for the artwork to keep away from any possible problems inside the destiny.

DO AVOID using random snap shots you decided on engines like google like google and yahoo or websites which encompass Pinterest. More regularly than not, the ones do now not include right attribution and are taken into consideration as stolen artwork. Should you make a decision to feature them to your designs and a person claims ownership over them, you can get your shop near down.

How to Create Your Merch

So, permit's say your request have been given authorised and you're now prepared to make your first shirt. How do you get started out? The actual advent method is an extended way extra sincere so you shouldn't have trouble setting a blouse collectively. Amazon even has templates to help you get the proper size on your layout so that you can region it to your shirt.

Here's what you want to do:

- Upload your PNG record for the layout and region it at the the front or once more of your shirt. You also can place on each aspects. Note which you'll want your document to be at three hundred PPI (pixels constant with inch) clearly so it appears appropriate even as Amazon prints it. If you're uncertain the manner to create the record or pick out out the proper period for it, bear in mind getting a 3rd-birthday party dressmaker that will help you out.

- Be conscious of putting your format on both elements of the shirt as this will up the charge of printing it and reduce your profits appreciably.

- Customize your shirt kind, its shade, and set the price.

- Provide data to your blouse. Give it a name, an Amazon title, and consist of an informative product description. Make effective you element out the dimensions, the sort of material, and some different element that a consumer might also want to understand.

- Finally, pick out out whether or not you need to sell through direct product link or in case you need to open it to the overall public. Choose the latter as this would allow Amazon's market to get right of entry in your shirt and buy it off of the internet site itself.

- Note that new debts will best be able to promote 10 first-rate shirts. This is what they speak with as "tier one". As you preserve, you'll sooner or later be upgraded to "tier " which then lets in you to promote 25 splendid shirts. As you go along with the float up a tier, the big form of shirts you could promote furthermore will increase. Note that you need now not create a modern day layout whenever. You can sell the same format 25 times and however circulate up.

Merch by means of using Amazon Fees

Before making a decision on a fee, undergo in mind the costs for promoting on Amazon Merch first. Doing so should assist make certain that you're not underpricing or overpricing your items.

- Price for the blouse. Note that placing better prices will cause a better payout for every object. However, shirts which can be too pricey will not sell as effects in contrast to others so you need to find out a specific stability among both.

- Type of blouse. You have alternatives: Anvil or Premium shirts. The Premium shirts do price $1.50 greater, however are of better excellent. Always pick out out the kind you understand your cutting-edge market base might appreciate.

- One-sided or double-sided. If you need to area your print on the back and front this can price you an extra $four.50. Tips for novices: if you're truly starting one and however getting a enjoy for the way subjects paintings, similarly to what will sell, opt for one-sided shirts first. This must hold the fee to a minimal and help you income higher, too.

As of 2017, the lowest price for the materials, the manufacturing and achievement for a shirt is $9.Eighty. Note that Amazon may also even price a 15% list fee for every product you positioned up.

Tips for Making a Sellable Shirt

- Color is a big element. Limit your shade alternatives to spherical three or 4, but make certain that every one fits your layout and does not overwhelm it. A little bit of coloration idea additionally enables—this would provide you with a tremendous idea of which colours complement every considered one of a type. Color could make or damage a brilliant format and render your shirt unsellable have to you arise a horrible mixture.

- Keep it easy. Don't make your shirt too "busy" with layers upon layers of design. The less tough designs promote the maximum. The equal goes for choosing shade. If a person desires more than 15 seconds to "apprehend" what's taking place with the design then you definately'll need to edit it.

- Symmetry. Of direction, you may want to stretch your creativity while designing shirts but do take note of the consumer's eye as properly. Balance is crucial, but asymmetrical designs aren't all that awful both. As prolonged as it's far accomplished artistically and tastefully, it may be definitely as thrilling and unique.

- Always consider your marketplace. Will you actually be selling cartoon shirts to those who are 30 years vintage and above? Know that Amazon's popular aim market is beneath 34 years of age so do your first-rate to cater to their taste, with out diluting your own mind as properly. Get opinions out of your pals and circle of relatives before placing out a format—a chunk of studies never harm.

Things to Avoid

- Do no longer use copyrighted and trademarked substances that don't belong to you in your designs.

- Do not use some element that violates global laws.

- Do not use pornographic fabric.

- Do no longer use something that promotes intolerance or hate.

- Do no longer use content cloth that exploits kids.

- Do no longer positioned up clean designs.

- Do no longer solicit remarks or evaluations to your gadgets.

- Be honest collectively along with your descriptions and make sure your products in form.

- Always create first-rate and expert designs.

- Never use the organization's name to suggest charitable or political features to your devices.

- Do not propose that your products have faster shipping at the same time as in comparison to others.

To observe greater about those, continuously undergo the terms and situations published with the resource of the use of the internet web website. It is important which you observe the regulations if you need to preserve your business enterprise employer and avoid all that attempt going to waste. Most of these are not unusual sense, except, and professional business company proprietors are nicely-privy to the quandary in terms of progressive license.

Remember, in case you're unsure—DON'T PUBLISH your design until you get the answers you want.

Chapter 6: Redbubble

Looking for a print on call for net website online wherein you've got got greater range in phrases of devices you could sell? Well, Redbubble might be the option you're looking for. This is a platform in which artists is probably able to add their very very own designs and get it posted on diverse items to promote.

About the Company

Artists earn coins via royalties, allowing them to gain about 20% of the income they set for every person item they promote on their pages. The rest of the cash then is going into production the items further to paying Redbubble's lessen.

Like a whole lot of precise POD net web sites, Redbubble handles each stock, deliver out, and transaction in your behalf. Artists will keep all of the rights to their designs so you need now not fear about inadvertently giving them permission to use your paintings somewhere else.

After uploading your art work one time, you could promote it on numerous gadgets for years and years. There's no expiration date at the designs you located up so if a selected one sells nicely? You can maintain taking benefit of it constantly. For artists who might be having hassle finding a manner to make cash for their art work, this is simply a terrific platform to begin on.

Not handiest can you are making a decent amount of passive profits through it, being on Redbubble and gaining an goal marketplace can also assist promote your art work. At the identical time, via the community, you'll additionally get to satisfy like-minded people and enlarge your network as nicely.

What Can You Sell On Redbubble

One of the standout matters approximately Redbubble is the quantity of products you may pick out from. Where a few PODs first-rate offer shirts and garb, Redbubble permits people to vicinity their designs on:

- Shirts

- Vinyl stickers

- Cases for incredible gadgets collectively with cell phones and capsules

Aside from these, you can moreover pick out to have your paintings printed on wall paintings and exclusive more realistic objects, making it appealing to humans of all ages. Here's what you can pick out from:

- Metal prints

- Greeting playing playing cards and postcards

- Framed prints and canvases

- Photographic prints

- Posters

- Calendar cover

- Calendar months

- Acrylic blocks

- Art prints

Note that your snap shots want to fulfill sure pixel sizes to hold them from turning into distorted for the duration of printing. There are guides provided on Redbubble's net net website, which have that will help you modify the photos as needed. Getting Started on Redbubble

The join up method is reasonably honest so novices shouldn't revel in any problem with getting began out. To assist you, however, here's a grade by grade guide to make sure the whole lot goes without problems.

- Open the internet net page's important web web page and click on on on "be a part of up". This is positioned on the pinnacle right nook of the internet page.

- Once you click on it, this could activate you to enter your e-mail, create a username, and post a password. Now, you can not edit your username later so choose a few factor that represents your business and sounds appealing to any ability consumer. Established artists must use their names, permitting enthusiasts and present customers to without problem discover them.

- After you end with join up, you'll circulate on to customizing your profile. The red and white icon at the pinnacle proper corner of the internet internet web page, showing a man with glasses will take you in your essential profile. From proper here, you could start tweaking it consistent with your opportunities.

- First, upload an icon or an avatar. You can also upload a cover photograph—basically, your maintain's banner and one of the first matters humans see when they go to your shop. Again, select out a few thing that now not only promotes your hold however additionally represents your merchandise properly. Do your incredible to make your internet net page aesthetically beautiful with complementing sun shades that in form your brand.

- Once accomplished, you may add a bio. This is in which you may provide statistics approximately yourself or about your industrial corporation. Try to jot down professionally without dropping your humorousness. Showing some character will gain you in terms of making rapport together together with your gift and extraordinary capability customers.

- Note that you could normally edit your profile so don't be afraid to check and mess around with it.

Useful Tools and Features Provided with the aid of RedBubble

One of the maximum useful abilties you can use at the internet website might be the "dashboard". This can also need to let you appearance simply how many human beings are viewing your paintings and what type of you are promoting. Included is a graph an amazing way to even provide you with data, displaying earnings with the aid of the date at the element of your top sellers. Use this to decide out just in which your customers are coming from, which of your advertising strategies are turning in, and the manner you may in addition improve your products.

The dashboard moreover comes with an pastime feed! This is a remarkable manner so you can see who is commenting in your merchandise, who is liking them, or maybe see what's up with the human beings you observe. Make fantastic you respond to any feedback you get professionally and keep up with the community so you're aware about what's trending.

Another beneficial characteristic could be "collections". This makes it on hand for purchasers to discover similar merchandise for your shop, in desire to scrolling thru person lists. It additionally makes your net web web page greater prepared and beautiful to everyone who might be surfing via it. Collections are generally focused on mediums and scenario maters, but you can categorize gadgets regular along with your alternatives.

For instance, you could create a "super provider" collection to help clients locate your most popular items. You can also create collections consistent with color, sort of product, or employer collectively items which have had priced cuts. To make a group:

- Click in your avatar placed at the pinnacle right nook.

- Go to "control profile" then create your new collection.

- To add a product to this organization, honestly select the gadgets and click on on the collections bar. Pick an gift collection or create a modern day one as wanted.

How to Upload Your Art on Redbubble

Now that you've familiarized yourself with how topics paintings, in addition to the first rate equipment you could use to make the whole lot greater accessible, it's time you uploaded your first layout. To do this, follow those smooth steps:

- Click in your avatar and pick "add new art work" from the dropdown menu. Make certain the photo has been properly sized and is in png layout before you add it. Unless you are importing a square photograph for gambling cards and posters, ensure your records obvious.

- Once uploaded, the interface will provide you sample alternatives for the picture. You also can exchange the history color for it so you can select one which fits nicely along side your layout.

- After you're accomplished with customizations, you could call the format and provide it an define. Make fine the info you embody are proper to the product. You also can upload some tags to help capacity customers discover your merchandise. For the ones tags, use phrases which you can in my view use for engines like google like google and yahoo.

- If your art work consists of a few mature content material, commonly ensure which you flag it earlier than publishing in any other case you risk getting it eliminated.

- After you're completed uploading, customizing, and which includes the critical descriptions—click on submit. This need to now seem to your profile whilst you refresh it.

Pricing and Marking Up Products

When pricing your devices, keep in mind this: base charge + your margin (how lots you need to earn from each sale) = your retail price. Redbubble permits its artist to have control over how heaps they promote their artwork for and what kind of of the complete rate they get to preserve. But, how do you decide on this?

- Most artists might also bump up the costs to their products with the beneficial aid of 35% as opposed to the common 20%. Now, this will appear like hundreds but if you're confident approximately your merchandise—without a doubt you wouldn't need to promote your self quick. Besides, if a person loves your artwork enough to buy it then they wouldn't mind paying more. If you're an artist who's counting on Redbubble to help your paintings and yourself, then that extra cash might be very useful.

- For artwork prints and stickers, there are artists who bump up the prices thru 50% if you need to in shape the expenses provided on specific print on call for internet websites. These are also smaller items and they regularly promote-out rapid—the few bucks you add wouldn't be too hefty. Just make sure each sticker is of awesome first-rate!

- Ask your self how masses you're inclined to pay for a tremendous object. If you would for my part purchase it for the price you have were given were given set then float for it. However, in case you anticipate it's too pricey—then decrease it. Remember, most of the human beings you're promoting to are normal people just like yourself. They, too, may also have budgets to take a look at and won't splurge on something so effects even though they love your paintings and you as an artist.

It moreover pays to do a piece of research earlier than setting a price. Look at comparable merchandise on other net web sites and check more about the fee differences. Doing this have that will help you discover a healthful balance, without compromising the charge of your precise paintings. Remember, don't underprice in reality to sell your merchandise. If you're not selling as lots as you concept inside the direction of the first few weeks—don't be involved. Just preserve marketing your devices and you'll discover your float.

Becoming Part of the Redbubble Community

We've set up the reality that Redbubble comes with a community in which artists can network with others and discover strategies to in addition beautify their artwork. Groups certainly play an crucial characteristic inside the Redbubble community and I pretty advocate becoming a member of a few even if you're new. To discover businesses at the manner to in shape your hobby, check those steps:

- Use the search bar and search for a subject that pursuits you. You'd be happy to comprehend that there are all kinds of companies to join. You can find out ones for one-of-a-kind art work mediums and techniques. There are ones for snap shots, for watercolor artists—even ones that focus on specific art subjects.

- Once you've determined a difficult and fast which you like, make certain that you have a have a look at via the policies in advance than making a post. Always be considerate of others within the identical group as you and have a look at any pointers they have got almost approximately posting pics.

These corporations may host disturbing situations, permitting their individuals to position up artwork that fits the given concept. The winners may want to take shipping of a spot at the institution's the the front internet page, boosting their publicity and assisting them all over again even greater lovers. I incredibly suggest novices to take part in those stressful situations—no longer best for the prize that carries it, but additionally to get comments and enhance their art work even more.

Tips on Marketing and Boosting Sales

Aside from turning into a member of companies and participating in challenges, artists can also widen their collect through on line advertising and marketing. There are many techniques via which this may be completed and proper right here are some to help you get began:

- Make use of social media. Share your artwork one in all a type structures in which you have were given developed a following—doesn't depend how huge or small the intention marketplace is. The component is to start and slowly get your call out there.

- Make use of Redbubble's advertising templates. Doing so makes the method of creating attractive commercials on your merchandise plenty extra available. This takes the guessing activity out what works and what doesn't—in particular if that is your first time making commercials.

- Wear your very very own merchandise! What higher way to get the phrase out and display off the amazing of your personal designs? Buy a couple of objects and make sure you use them often. It is probably that a person will ask in which you obtain them from and you'll be capable of point them on your hold.

If you have got a chunk of cash to spare, why not buy some of your non-public merchandise to use as samples? Some people aren't comfortable with buying gadgets they haven't seen in individual so this is one way to introduce them to what you're promoting.

- Think about growing corporation playing cards that embody your Redbubble web page. If you should make a stable enterprise out of this opportunity, would possibly as well deal with it professionally. The identical is going for linking your shop web page to some different social media payments you've got got, whether that be Instagram or twitter. If you have a separate net web web page to your paintings, ensure that you link your store on it as nicely! Doing this now not best allows with advertising and advertising, however additionally establishes your popularity—making your products greater appealing to potential customers.

Chapter 7: Kindle Publishing

The net has in reality change the manner many industries and masses of human beings do their business enterprise. Among them, the publishing worldwide has visible the maximum significant—wherein authors might want to go through publishing homes so as to get their paintings obtainable, the net has leveled the playing area and enabled writers to put up their paintings thru using themselves. No 1/3 events and basically retaining a bigger percent of the overall income.

In reality, these days, you want no longer be a first rate-selling creator to make a decent earnings on-line. Any idea may be modified right into a book and even the commonplace man or woman can publish one. There are many options via which this can be completed, however one of the most popular for every experts and novices alike would be Amazon Publishing.

About the Company

Through Amazon's Kindle, you may self-post your ebook and start earning earnings inner 24-hours. Compare that to the months or years that it could on occasion take an writer to ultimately get their e-book into print. Amazon itself is a famous and first rate corporation. They presently have over ninety million subscribers on Prime and that's inside the United States on my own. You can without a doubt don't forget how massive and global its attain certainly is.

When you parent with Kindle Direct Publishing, you moreover mght get to maintain extra of the income. Did I point out that publishing through this platform may be completed without charge to you? Amazon has democratized publishing, allowing non-writers to put up art work regardless of its scenario count number. You can write:

- Fiction

- Non-fiction

- Historical portions

- Biographies

- Children's books

- Young individual books

- Travel books

- Memoirs

- Self-help books

- Guide books

- Travel books

- Cooking books

And so on. What sincerely counts so as with a purpose to profits is that there's an target audience for the ebook you're writing. Given the kind of humans the usage of Amazon to browse new picks every single day—you may bet there'll constantly be a reader who is looking for precisely what you want to offer.

The stats don't lie. According to Author Earnings, there's over 485, 538,000 e-books being supplied on Amazon—published via way of round 20,000 man or woman authors. Needless to mention, if writing is more your velocity whilst compared to virtual art work, then that is a market you may want to tap into. You need not be JK Rowling so that you can make coins through writing. The only property you need are creativity, a very particular or informative idea, and a platform that in which you could start selling your e book.

What Kind of Books Sell Best on Amazon?

- If you haven't any concept wherein to start, begin through way of surfing the website's bestseller list. On there, you'll discover what topics sell the maximum and feature the exceptional income capability. You can placed your very private spin on it and make it surely years—then begin advertising and advertising and advertising and marketing and advertising and marketing.

- Another hassle you may strive is spotting "gaps" or topics that are not nicely blanketed with the resource of what's presently at the listing. Doing this will require extra research for your aspect near writing the e book, mainly if you aren't familiar with the concern. However, this will show to be very profitable— there absolutely might be a large marketplace searching beforehand to what you're going to put in writing down.

- Do you want to install writing lengthy books at the manner to make a earnings? Absolutely now not! You can write shorter books that focus on a selected situation take into account and nevertheless make respectable profits. Of course, you'll need to price a miles lower rate for the ones. In reality, books priced amongst $2.Ninety nine and $four.Ninety nine frequently make the maximum sales.

Types of Self-Publishing on Amazon

You can choose amongst publishing posted books and eBooks whilst you be part of up for this software. Below, we communicate the professionals and cons of each.

- eBooks

This is taken into consideration to be the maximum fee-effective manner of self-publishing on the Amazon platform. Given that it's miles virtual, people may be able to right away download the e-book onto their devices—alongside aspect the Kindle eBook reader. You can without issue do that thru the Kindle Direct Publishing software program software, that is virtually free to apply. Meaning, there's no want to make investments any cash earlier than you could start taking off eBooks. You will want an Amazon account, of path.

The blessings of this software consists of:

•The capability to feature your ebook onto the platform inner only a few mins. After that, your ebook ought to be available inside the marketplace interior multiple days.

•You will maintain all of the rights to your content material material fabric and be capable of select your very very very own fee for what you upload.

•Each time you sell a ebook, you will be able to pocket 70% of its total sale charge and Amazon will hold the relaxation.

•Want to edit some element on a published ebook? You'll be capable of do absolutely that at any given time. Once you're accomplished, you can honestly resubmit your paintings and put up it yet again.

The excellent drawback proper here is the reality that some human beings pick having bodily copies of the books they purchase. In this regard, you'll possibly isolate a number of the humans looking for published copies and lose some earnings over it.

- Printed Books

Want to have a physical reproduction of your tough art work that you can proudly show at home or provide to pals as gadgets? You have that choice as well and it's far called "print-on-call for". This allows authors to supply paperback versions in their art work and is available through the Kindle Direct Publishing software. This is specially first rate for promoting greater copies as there are lots of those who select physical books over digital ones.

That stated, there are variations amongst digital and non-digital publishing. For example, instead of pocketing 70% of the income, it'll be decreased to 60%. Not a horrible quantity, of path, however have a look at that Amazon will take out publishing charges for each sale which you make. Another crucial interest is the cover of your ebook—a whole lot of humans pay special attention to how a book appears and this elements into whether or now not or now not they'll buy it or not. If you haven't any historic beyond in designing covers, you may opt to get a 3rd birthday party to help you out with it.

Can you offer each a virtual and revealed replica of your e-book? YES you could. Doing this could beautify your earnings at the same time as now not having to do additional paintings.

Creating Your First Book on Amazon

Though the machine is quite sincere, you'll need to make sure you do topics correctly to avoid any troubles afterward. To help you get began out right, proper here's a little by little guide.

- Writing and formatting your ebook

After you have got got written your e-book, it's time you centered on polishing it. Note that Amazon has very strict requirements in terms of mistakes so make sure it's far written nicely. Mind the length of your ebook, dispose of what may be removed, and edit and passages that might be difficult to have a have a look at.

Next to writing, enhancing is crucial to generating super content cloth cloth that human beings will experience reading. Remember, this is meant to be presented— for people to pay particular cash for what you need to offer, it should be provided nicely.

If you've got extra cash to spare, recollect getting a 3rd birthday celebration that will help you with improving earlier than publishing.

- Create your Kindle Direct Publishing account

Next, you want to create your KDP account. You may be asked to your personal facts. You can choose to enter your call or the call you've got got given your impartial publishing commercial enterprise corporation. They may additionally even ask on your cope with, zip code, smartphone number, and e-mail address. Note that Amazon will rent this records to deliver you any vital notifications at a few degree within the booklet of your e-book.

Amazon can even gather tax facts from you, which encompass your individual taxpayer identification, and your social safety variety. This is done for use in coping with taxes in addition to any royalty price when you begin making earnings out of your books.

Already have an Amazon account? Then you may use your present login information, if you desire, to create a today's KDP profile.

- Select your e-book layout

As , you have got alternatives for this. Consider which one fits the shape of ebook you recommend on promoting—does it enchantment greater to paperback creditors or does some thing a piece more cellular and reachable fit higher? Note that you can continuously promote your e-book in each codecs to similarly enhance your income.

- Proper formatting to your ebook

If you've written your e-book the usage of giant word processors which consist of Microsoft Word, word that you could must layout it properly simply so it displays well at the Kindle e-reader and on its paperback form. Fortunately, doing this has moreover been made clean—Amazon offers authors with guides on the manner to prep your e book with as plenty tons much less trouble as possible. Just look for the mentioned instructional on the net website to get started!

How to Create a Book Listing

- Start thru getting access to your bookshelf for your KDP account. Through this, you may be capable of add your e-book in addition to create your listings. You'll furthermore be edit your current-day listings and test your character stats using this dashboard. To add your completed paintings, click on on on "+ Kindle eBook" or "+ Paperback" relying at the format you pick out.

- Add your ebook records. Once you have your ebook uploaded, you'll be asked to offer data about it and approximately yourself as properly. This includes the basics, together with the name of your e book, an outline for it, the best age variety, and your call amongst different topics.

Note that this is in which you'll be able to add a few identifying instructions and key phrases which ought to assist your supposed goal marketplace discover your e-book. For example, in case your e book is ready traveling then ensure you upload that unique keyword and listing it in that unique class.

Take a while with this step and double take a look at the whole lot you write down. The extra entire your list is, the better your possibilities at getting your e-book located via the right marketplace.

- Create a cover to your book. If you've got got already were given an picture, one which you very own the copyright to, then ensure it's the proper length earlier than uploading. You moreover have the option of designing your own the use of the internet net web page's included characteristic as a way to guide you through the approach of creating one yourself.

Make notable your cover is appealing and balanced—one so as to make readers curious and gives humans with a visual summary of what your e-book might be about. Other key subjects to bear in mind, encompass:

•Amazon shows making cover images which have a top and width ration of one:6

•You can opt to rent a person to do the format for you. The greater expert your e-book appears, the greater appealing it'll possibly be to capacity customers. When it includes publishing, first impressions continuously matter quantity!

- Uploading your e-book. KDP will take shipping of awesome document codecs, which includes PDDF, DOC, HTML, and mobi. Just make certain your content material cloth follows the right Kindle format, otherwise it received't seem nicely as soon as published.

Submitting Your Work for Publishing

Ready to make your ebook to be had for anyone to shop for? Before you hit "submit", comply with the steps beneath just so you may be pleasant that you're presenting all of your hard art work inside the pleasant way possible.

- Always preview your cover layout, similarly in your internet web page format. Make use of the net internet website's preview characteristic so you can test if your completed e-book appears precise and if the entirety is in region. Use this opportunity to double take a look at for any typos and formatting errors. Note that if you're getting your ebook physically discovered, that is your last chance to repair any mistakes.

•EBooks are displayed in a one-of-a-kind way on one in every of a kind video display units. Do use numerous devices to look if your e-book appears ok across the board—if not, constantly restoration this in advance than publishing. You need to provide your readers the fine viable revel in on the equal time as analyzing via your book.

- Setting a fee for your ebook. First off, the price you offer your ebook need to be truthful and need to take into account the marketability of its issue count number and its format. Basically, it's miles first-class proper to price greater for a posted paperback on English literature at the identical time as in evaluation to a quick eBook approximately essential pix. To gain a higher idea, take a look at titles much like your ebook and have a look at their pricing.

•Note that you could select amongst 70% and 35% when it comes to your royalty options. The higher the fee will help enhance your profits. If you're selling physical copies, there may be no delivery charge if you only claim 35%. For authors who've a smaller marketplace, this is probably the better choice. A charge decrease than $2.99 will inspire higher sales.

•Amazon will deduct a sure percentage from each sale. This is referred to as a distribution charge.

- Publish your ebook. Once you're satisfied and feature checked that the entirety's in order, it's time to post what you've been jogging tough on. The documents you previously uploaded with be sent to KDP or to the CreateSpace content material material material group—the ones are the individuals who will prep it for print ebook. You may be sent a notification as speedy as your ebook is available on the internet website online.

•How prolonged does it generally take? It typically takes seventy hours for books to turn out to be organized for buy through Amazon. Note that you'll be able to edit and replace your listing, even after the ebook has been published.

Remember, you received't make cash proper away after publishing. In reality, it may take weeks as a way to make a sale. However, in case you marketplace your e-book and keep pushing its visibility, you may enhance your profits and flip your tough paintings right into a achievement. The paintings doesn't prevent upon publishing— you need to hold selling your self as and writer along with the usefulness of your books.

Chapter 8: Niche Affiliate Marketing

Imagine searching for to sell each product you believe you studied can also sell to anybody in the marketplace—sounds hard, proper? There's additionally pretty some drawbacks to doing this, specially the amount of opposition you'll be coping with. Fact is: if a product is promoting well, every person else will soar on that bandwagon.

So why no longer select some thing particular and promote that to a smaller section of the marketplace, but with a more danger of correctly making sales? Not high-quality do you efficaciously reduce the amount of competition you've got got, you furthermore mght create an opportunity for yourself in terms of cornering that precise marketplace.

Building a Niche Affiliate Marketing Website

The idea proper here is to locate your niche, get suitable ratings on Google for the critical element terms you've determined on, and turn all that website website traffic into income through your partner promotions. So, permit's preserve this clean:

- Start through discovering niche thoughts. The more unique it's miles, the better—however do ensure there may be a exquisite market for it. Make a brief list of thoughts then undergo it another time until you locate a true candidate to your niche.

- Next up, key-word studies. It's certainly easy to surely go with the number one related trouble that includes thoughts, however if you're to succeed? You want to transport more in-depth. Find out what people in that region of hobby are looking for—listing down specific key phrases and a few famous ones as well. You ought to want to apply an remarkable aggregate of the 2; keep in mind it as getting the fantastic of both worlds.

- Make your net web page stand out. What problems will your internet internet site assist with fixing? Are you offering some thing specific?

- Pick a website name—choose one that represents your business enterprise properly, but is also catchy. Take some time with this one because of the fact frequently changing it isn't always wonderful pricey, but can also tarnish your recognition as a web marketer.

- Find strong net host with packages that you could manage to pay for. It all is predicated upon upon your price range, in reality, but beginners must pick the primary plans till money starts offevolved coming in.

- Think approximately designing a logo and selecting a pleasing, easy problem keep in mind for your internet site. Keep matters professional and nicely-prepared. Your companion links want to be the front and middle, however not too-in-your face that your web page traffic get grew to become off thru them. As heaps as feasible, preserve the entirety herbal and insert the links in which they healthy terrific. Do keep away from overly busy pages with too many things moving or blinking—simplicity is essential. - Content is king. Do your exquisite to enlarge a long term content cloth technique—one that is sustainable and possible for you. You can write your personal if you have loose time, however as quickly as your net website starts offevolved offevolved raking in internet web page visitors? You may need to maintain in thoughts getting a third birthday celebration do it for you.

- Pick your preferred monetization approach. For this, you may take a look at out some of the options to be had to you— discover what fits your needs nice and which one you're maximum snug with.

- Link constructing. The oldest trick within the e book—however now not precisely the very excellent each. The concept is to growth visibility for your website on line thru including it to on line directories or linking up with distinct associated web websites.

- Make use of social media. If you have a following on Facebook, Twitter, Instagram, and one in all a kind big social media systems—make sure you hyperlink your website to those pages. Even if you don't have a sizeable following, hyperlink it up anyway. This facilitates raise your visibility and moreover establishes your popularity on line. Remember: the wider your reach, the better.

Joining Niche Networks and Its Benefits

There are many associate applications to be had that the mere act of selecting one may be daunting. Which one suits you superb? Which ones will assist you generate a constant passive profits? For the ones in the region of hobby enterprise, a gap network truely works top notch. Here's what you need to recognise:

- With vicinity of interest networks, you'll discover merchandise which might be most applicable to your internet website online multi function place. This lessens the amount of time you will have invested into searching. All you need to do is leaf through the options, find the outstanding fits, then take a look at conversion and charge rates for each software software.

- Most area of interest networks moreover provide more competitive fee charges while compared to the common accomplice network. Instead of the regular 10%, area of interest networks can provide you 30% - 50% of the general profits profit.

Why? This is due to the fact the networks apprehend how profitable their specific place of hobby is—that's precisely why they set the network up. In unique, programs related weight reduction, creating a dwelling, health, intercourse, and courting are taken into consideration evergreen due to the fact there's commonly a market for it.

- You can be able to art work with associate managers who've revel in if you need to seriously assist you in navigating the place of interest. These managers apprehend the products and the marketplace itself in a extra enormous way, allowing them to help you maximize your conversions and sales and what data you need to encompass for your website to simply improve your earnings. For a newbie? This is in reality beneficial.

Chapter 9: Youtube Affiliate Marketing

By now, it might be that you've heard of companion marketing and advertising and what it is. It's one of the most customarily used techniques for people to make some passive earnings online. Compared to different options, it is also quite clean and on hand to maximum. That stated, did you recognize that you may use this identical concept and apply it to honestly one in every of the most important content material material material introduction platform we've proper now? YouTube affiliate advertising is an possibility you actually wouldn't want to overlook out on.

About The Company

On YouTube, you may find out a network of like-minded people sharing mind and video content. The sort of topics range extensively—some thing from gardening, splendor, home décor, adventure, and so on. Needless to mention, there's a few component for quite an entire lot everyone.

Aside from being a treasure trove of facts and thoughts, it can moreover be a profitable marketplace for any associate marketer. The system of associate marketing and marketing on YouTube essentially follows the equal video content material fabric material advent idea, but with the addition of placing companion links in the video itself via the use of annotations or thru video descriptions.

It in fact is that easy—no exceptional from inclusive of your links to a blogpost or to your social media pages. If some detail, YouTube lets in you to be greater modern and resourceful with what video you pick out to create, in addition to the manner you need to offer the goods or offerings you are selling.

In reality, many content material creators at the platform are already doing this in some form. There is, but, a difference among the professional marketers and the informal entrepreneurs. You can tell the distinction with the useful aid of the manner nicely-produced the movies are.

- The professional marketers have a propensity to be "spammier", generating video after video with nearly identical content material just to decorate their associate commissions. You'll locate that their content material cloth also simplest revolves round selling the goods— there's a obvious lack of interplay with the network.

- The casual marketers are crafted from generally average people whose channels revolve round their specific vicinity of interest or statistics. They produce videos alleged to entertain or tell—with the occasional companion hyperlink to sell a product they might be playing within the propose time. They furthermore have interaction with the community extra, constructing a stable target market as they gain this.

How to Make Money via YouTube Affiliate Marketing

First off, you need to determine out what kind of films truly paintings for this motive. Like we've installed in advance, there are various precise patterns and codecs. Here are some examples of what may paintings fine for accomplice advertising and advertising.

- Product Reviews

Comparison films or single product evaluations have a quite unique target market base on YouTube. This layout also lends itself properly to the cause of affiliate advertising and marketing, permitting you to vicinity up hyperlinks for the goods you'll be reviewing in your channel in order that your subscribers need to get to attempt it too.

It is a truth that many people watch overview films earlier than growing a purpose and approximately fifty two% are much more likely to buy a product after it has been featured in a YouTube evaluate. Needless to say, that may be a win-win state of affairs for every stores and entrepreneurs. Allowing each events to earn revenue through the platform.

- DIY Videos

Got masses of thoughts for own family hacks and various useful DIYs? Well, why now not bear in thoughts sharing the ones on YouTube? Not first-class can you help exclusive people via the ones informative home home home windows, it's moreover a terrific way to signify merchandise by means of the use of way of the use of associate hyperlinks.

If you consider you studied an object can be beneficial for a specific undertaking, placed a link to wherein human beings can purchase it—doing so lets in them on the same time as you earn a chunk of rate as well.

- Top 10 Videos / Best Of Videos

Now, the trick proper right here is to assemble a reputation for yourself as an professional on this rely. It may additionally even help to recognition on a selected hassle, collectively with own family gadgets or vehicle add-ons. Even with just a unmarried situation count number, you can create numerous movement pix even as not having to compromise the extremely good of your paintings.

Any product protected to your listing ought to have an associated accomplice link—that on my own can earn you a remarkable quantity of revenue relying on how large your reap is.

Getting Affiliate Links

You'd be happy to recognise that almost each single employer or logo runs some form of partner software program. This manner you'll have hundreds of picks other than Amazon. You can test out companies together with Target, Wal-Mart, and Best Buy— actually do a clean Google are searching for or studies if a enterprise you're hobby in selling has a software that you may be part of. That stated, maintain the subsequent in thoughts:

- Choose agencies that go with the precept recognition of your channel. Remember, you're now not without a doubt selling random merchandise proper proper here. What you're linking desires to attraction for your audience as properly. So, in case your channel generally focuses on visiting recommendations then find out partner programs associated with adventure and journey tools. Just bear in mind having a splendor-based completely channel with associate links for kitchen resources—it doesn't fit and could honestly confuse your target market.

- Learn extra about the brand you're selling. Do their ideals align with yours? Make positive that this is so due to the fact you wouldn't need to inadvertently promote merchandise from a commercial enterprise organisation that isn't professional. Your name and your very own popularity is at stake, anyhow.

- Price variety. Again, bear in mind your goal marketplace and the location of interest marketplace you'll be selling to. Say your intention are humans in their early twenties who're already running or balancing artwork with their studies. You wouldn't want to try to promote them high-priced brands— you're not going to make any profits from that. Always, healthful your target market to the products you choose to promote.

- You can use companion links for the similar products however from special producers. This is specially so if you're a evaluation channel—you may provide your goal market with options that allows you to decide for themselves which one they choose best.

Once you've located the right packages for yourself, all that's left to do is sign up and set-up your account. Different groups have wonderful sign on techniques so make certain you look at every properly and provide the precise statistics at the same time as requested.

Getting Started with Affiliate Marketing on YouTube

Opening an account with YouTube is easy— you could actually have your non-public already. However, if you're starting off a personal logo, it might be nice to start from scratch. So, for the novices—right right here's what you need to do:

- Prepare your YouTube account. The signal-up gadget for YouTube is straightforward, in fact make certain the information you provide fits what you want your identification to be on the platform. What this shows is:

•Do you need to use your personal call or might you as an opportunity be recognized for the call of your logo. Choosing the various two sincerely is primarily based upon at the shape of channel you'll have. I recommend going with the brand and truely introducing yourself for your target audience through the films and channel description.

•Note that there's a geared up period in case you need to exchange your channel call so make certain you supply it a terrific one to your first try.

- Next, customize your channel. YouTube allows creators to characteristic an avatar and a banner to make your channel reflect you as a person in any other case you as a emblem. Other topics you could add, embody:

•Links for your social media pages! Don't forget about those as they may assist establish your reputation greater.

•Profile. You need not write a prolonged biography—in reality provide all the essential statistics which encompass your name, what your channel is ready, and what people can expect.

•Links to related channels. YouTube could usually listing the most comparable ones in your channel, however you can additionally favor to manually link ones of your choosing.

Start Uploading Affiliate Marketing Videos

The key-phrase proper here is: professionalism and great work. You need no longer be an professional video editor to gather this, but you'll need to take a look at a bit if this is your first time growing a YouTube video. Below are some suggestions:

- Find a video editing software program software which you're comfortable with. There are free and paid apps to pick out from, but the maximum critical is finding one that is straightforward to apply but produces excellent effects. You ought to in all likelihood need to look into what different Youtubers are using.

- Simplify your equipment. What does a median content author need? A terrific digital camera, precise lighting fixtures, and tremendous audio recording system. I recommend taking pictures trial motion snap shots earlier than diving headfirst into your first manufacturing. Find out what works and what doesn't—but don't make things too complicated. If you're a one man or woman operation, make certain you could deal with all of the artwork with out a fantastic deal trouble.

- Spontaneous or scripted? Some human beings do better while talking on a topic with out following a script. However, for novices, it's far encouraged that you define all the belongings you need to speak about for your motion snap shots. This may make the whole lot extra organized and your target audience can be able to have a look at the statistics you're giving with out problems.

- Give your videos titles containing particular key phrases that your ability target marketplace is probably searching for. Use the hashtags as nicely—those will help decorate visibility to your channel and your content material.

- Last however no longer the least, in which do you upload your associate links? It is traditional workout for humans to encompass it of their video descriptions or in video annotations. Just bear in mind of how many hyperlinks you add for your description—you wouldn't need humans clicking away in advance than completing your video. Remember, those films may be monetized as nicely!

Balance is pinnacle right right here. You want to establish a popularity, benefit an intention market, and make all of that sustainable. At the same time, you have to moreover prioritize what you really want— is it getting your movies to rank or getting people to shop for thru your accomplice links. Of route, every is probably finished but it will require more strive out of your prevent.

Chapter 10: Instagram Affiliate Marketing

Known as of the most vital social media systems, Instagram offers people an untapped opportunity for earning passive profits online. This is some component you could take gain of, but first—you need to analyze the way.

How does it Work?

It's no extraordinary from more conventional approach of associate advertising and marketing and marketing. To earn cash via it, a person (in this situation, a social media influencer) should installation a partnership with a agency's associate software. From there, they will hire their social media debts to put up and sell approximately the agency's merchandise—advertising it to their following and incomes fee on every sale related to that submit.

Is it worthwhile? The answer is YES, however so as for it to reveal up any income—you need to apprehend the way to maximise the platform's functionality first. For instance, you can not encompass a link every time you put up a photograph and people links are key to being an associate. How else will you be capable of sell a agency or a product?

For this, you've got got got a few options:

- Permanent link in your bio.

Given that this is one of the first subjects humans see at the same time as looking through your Instagram internet internet page, it first-rate makes feel to place your associate hyperlink right right here. If you're selling some thing via a post, all you want to do is tell human beings to locate and click on on on the link on your bio. This is specially quality in case you're absolutely working for one precise emblem.

- Semi-permanent link to your bio.

Want to work with particular affiliates so that you can switch up the goods you're recommending? For this reason, semi-everlasting links in your bio might also want to artwork extremely good. In order to make this artwork, you may want to update the link whenever you are making a trendy merchandising positioned up—which makes it a bit tedious and additionally likely tough to your intention marketplace.

See, in the event that they discover any products out of your older posts thrilling they wouldn't be redirected to the right internet web page inside the event that they click on on in your bio link. Needless to say, it isn't the maximum green manner of doing subjects however it can paintings if you don't make normal accomplice posts.

- Linkable Instagram gallery app.

For this, you can use services consisting of Linkin.Bio or Link2But which allows people and brands to installation a digital hold. This is basically just like your Instagram gallery, however with clickable posts as a way to steer humans in your partner links. Whilst it is to be had and offers your promotional posts in an less difficult and similarly curated, be aware that now not all of us may be snug with clicking away from your profile to open yet any other page.

- Swipe-up Instagram stories.

This isn't a feature that's really to be had for each Instagram customer, however if you have a enterprise account with fanatics starting from 10,000 and above then you need to be able to see the swipe-up link choice to your Instagram reminiscences. Using this makes it simpler on your enthusiasts to view the submit and click on the hyperlink which might deliver them in your partner's web page.

The satisfactory downsides right here are the truth that novices will no longer be capable of take benefit of this option and industrial agency debts do usually generally tend to get a good deal much less engagement on the platform in assessment to personal ones.

Establishing Your Account and Promoting It

- Already have a private account that you want to reveal proper right into a business?

Well, you want to begin growing your follower count variety. See, numbers do anticipate Instagram—it may no longer be the most critical motive why manufacturers could possibly need to artwork with human beings but it does issue into topics.

To construct an active following, make certain you have got interaction with human beings inside your network. Follow comparable payments, observation without a doubt in photographs, and widen your community as you development. Simply following 10 to fifteen bills an afternoon and leaving 10 or greater comments an afternoon will help boom the eye in the direction of your business enterprise profile.

- Make use of hashtags—sparingly.

This is how humans find exquisite posts on the platform and the usage of it right can help make your promotional posts more seen to those who might be inquisitive about it. Sure, the way is quite gradual and it would make an effort for you to in truth advantage fans thru it. However, the approach can't be virtually dismissed. It's first-class a depend of being clever with how you use it.

Research is top in this example. You want to discover the proper hashtags to use in your precise niche. Be conscious of:

•Which ones are very energetic and function quite some people following it?

•Which ones are oversaturated, in which your posts will be buried by others within a few minutes?

•Which ones have masses of engagement?

When you operate hashtags, keep it to no less than 5 to ten unique ones. There is the sort of factors as too many and you will need to keep away from giving your target marketplace the effect that you're simplest on the platform to make money.

- Host contests and giveaways.

Even if you're a particularly small account, web web hosting smooth giveaways can assist beautify your follower rely and your visibility. The idea need to be saved smooth, but no plenty a whole lot less appealing for your current consumer pool and in your potential clients. Below are a few recommendations:

•Keep your reward workable. It might be a reduction voucher, a web present card, or an informative eBook. What topics is that it may be brought to the winner with out problem and with out costing too much. Do supply out a couple of price—if there's a extra risk of people winning, they're much more likely to participate in it.

•Create clean guidelines that advantage you and your business agency. For instance: make certain that human beings are following your Instagram account and are tagging friends inside the comments to your giveaway submit.

Think of this as phrase-of-mouth advertising and marketing with a twist. By having others tag their pals to your posts, you're able to widen your advantage and capture the attention of functionality clients. By requiring them to have a observe if you want to qualify for the prize, you are also boosting your follower be counted.

- Clean up your account and make certain it shows your brand.

Aesthetics have end up increasingly critical—particularly for an photo primarily based platform which encompass Instagram. You can't absolutely publish what you need; it is vital that your privy to what you're importing, the way it makes your net web page look, what it represents, and what impact it offers people who are viewing your net page.

Branding is vital and you'll want to offer your enterprise properly as a way to live aggressive and relevant. For this, recollect:

•Creating a topic remember in your Instagram net web page. It can be some trouble as simple as following a particular color scheme or posting snap shots that have a comparable problem. The more cohesive your web page is, the greater attractive it will become to the individual viewing it.

•Choose charming text and add relatable content material cloth cloth. It's now not constantly about enterprise—people want to peer a extra human element on your net web page. This makes you more relatable and they'll be much more likely to take a look at your product pointers with more take delivery of as real with.

- Sponsored posts.

Whether you're a beginner or had been at it for some time, backed posts can simply help you assemble a following. The top notch bit approximately that is Instagram will simply allow you to choose which vicinity of hobby hobby and which demographic you want to intention with this backed advert. This method only your focused market will see it, helping improve its effectiveness.

Since you may be identifying to shop for this service, it's far exquisite to make sure which you are becoming your coins's well really really worth. Choose your most well-known post for this cause, in particular the most effective with the most amount of engagement. You handiest have some seconds to lure their hobby and pique their interest so you'll want a put up that has examined so that it will reaching that.

A few tips:

•Opt for vibrant shades and formidable text.

•Don't make your image too busy and complicated. It has to deliver the message truely and definitely.

•Using a version for the photo? Make sure they do no longer overpower the message you're trying to deliver. Also, in order a terrific way to keep away from getting suspended, handiest use pictures which you very own the copyright to.

•Videos vs. Still photographs. Both have its specialists and cons, however no matter the reality that photos were established to be greater effective almost about drawing in humans's interest.

•Landscape or portrait. Fun reality: portrait pictures have been identified to be higher for growing commercials in fashionable due to the reality they hire the space better and you may do extra seeing that you have were given a larger canvas to play with.

Instagram is offers associates with a terrific possibility for passive profits. There are masses of heaps of customers with one-of-a-kind pursuits that you could tap into. Of route, fulfillment will no longer are available a unmarried day however follow the pointers furnished above and I can guarantee you of an extremely good begin.

Remember, you have to hooked up effort and time—a few issue that want to be done each day and with consistency. You'll begin seeing the pay-off in no time.

Chapter 11: Ebates Referral Program

Everybody loves an excellent cashback software program—it lets in with saving a piece of cash whenever we hold. But what's amazing approximately the Ebates referral utility is that apart from getting cashback out of your purchases, you can additionally earn more via referring a friend to enroll in and emerge as a member.

How does it Work?

The idea is for modern-day members to unfold the word approximately this system. If you efficiently refer a chum who then makes a qualified buy—each of you may earn a reward. Note that the desired buy and amount for the praise does range masses, so maintain your self up to date thru their "refer-a-pal" web page for any adjustments.

To get started out:

- If you're already an Ebates member, all you want to do is get your unique referral link. This is to be had thru the refer-a-buddy net web page. If you're now not but a member, you need to join up first as a way to take gain of this possibility.

- Once you've got got your personal link, you can then supply it for your buddies and circle of relatives. You can use text messaging, social media, messaging apps, or even electronic mail. The critical component proper here is they click on your link and sign up for a membership through it.

- The hyperlink may be very important due to the truth that is how Ebates is probably monitoring in fact how many a success referrals you have controlled.

- Note that your buddy want no longer make a buy right away. They have inside a 12 months of signing as lots as make the qualifying buy so each of you can earn a reward.

- How soon will you got your bonus? This is commonly despatched inside 60 days, after your referral efficiently makes the qualifying buy.

How a first-rate deal are you capable of earn for every a success referral you're making? Well, if your certified referral makes a complete of $25 in purchases inner a three hundred and sixty five days of them registering, you could get maintain of $five as a base bonus. This won't look like plenty, but if you get 10 humans to join up and purchase something? That's $50 immediately into your pocket with out a bargain attempt.

There are a few crucial subjects to preserve in mind while referring humans the use of your hyperlink. Be aware of the following:

- A certified referral handiest counts if it's made through the precise hyperlink you obtain from the internet site.

- The referral need to be for the common individual—this means that that registering corporations and criminal entities will no longer depend towards the reward.

- Avoid posting your referral hyperlink on an Ebates service provider's social media bills or every different online presence. Some people will try this as a manner to growth the form of their referrals—but that may be a black hat technique and need to be prevented. You can get your membership revoked need to you be caught doing this.

- You also can be disqualified from earning the bonuses through growing blogs and net pages which have your link on them. The identical is going for dispensing your precise hyperlink through bulk e mail or every other method that can be taken into consideration as junk mail.

How Can You Make Money from The Referral Program?

With all the above in mind, it'd look like growing a living thru this application may be difficult. This is not the case, but, and all you really want to do is be clever approximately the way you technique matters. Remember, you'll best get disqualified if you put up your specific link in pages that aren't yours. So, right right here's what you can do:

- Have a weblog? Use it. First off, curate your older weblog posts and find out ones wherein you can insert a link selling this system. Do you have got got articles about the way to make coins at domestic? Share your hyperlink. What approximately posts on merchandise that might be available via the Ebates software? If there are any, update those as nicely.

- You also can pick to create attractive new content material. After all, who wouldn't be inquisitive about a software program that not brilliant offers people cashback within the course of purchasing— however furthermore presents them with a manner to earn coins? Remember, preserve it conversational and be as goal as viable. Don't push the club onto anybody—in case you spotlight all of the advantages, you can make certain that they'll join up without in addition want for convincing.

- Use your electronic mail list. Are you the type to "acquire" emails out of your very very own buddies and pals? Well, it's time to make use of that and invite them to the Ebates software software. Much like writing blog posts, ensure your invitation is conversational and now not pushy. People are much more likely to enroll in a few component if you preserve topics pleasant in desire to blatantly company-like.

- Lastly, use your social media presence. There are a few techniques to try this, however I discover posting about the products you need to shop for your self then casually bringing up the Ebates software program application works excellent. It receives humans curious enough to join up the usage of the unique hyperlink.

Note that much like all of the particular options from this listing, the referral application will no longer make you right away richer. However, it's far a likely shape of passive profits online and can be maximized in case you located in the extra attempt to accomplish that. It's all approximately how an entire lot time you truely invest into it and the manner creative you may get approximately selling this tool itself.

Chapter 12: What Is Passive Income?

Passive Income is possibly the maximum awesome manner to earn coins in the twenty first Century. Why, you ask? Because it consists of a top notch deal less try and exceptional returns. There isn't any shortcut to turning into wealthy. But there may be a "clever reduce". It instructions smart paintings instead of difficult paintings. With accurate steerage and backbone, you may be capable of format a moneymaker that would print coins on the same time as you sleep. I understand you're intrigued, but first, permit us to recognize what passive income is.

Introduction to Passive Income

In easy phrases, passive profits is a shape of earnings that requires very little attempt to upkeep. A very not unusual example of passive earnings is condominium profits in which you rent your house in exchange for cash. Neither does it require your whole-time involvement nor does it require an entire lot of upkeep. The save you stop quit end result is that you purchased an superb quantity of extra cash with out breaking an awful lot sweat.

Passive income is much like the tale of "The Golden Goose." You ought to be affected man or woman and no longer permit greed come in the way of making a sustainable model. I advocate you to understand passive income as an prolonged-term asset rather than a short-time period profits maker. If you control to earn a tremendous profits on the begin, your consciousness want to be to invest it. Investing is a first-rate way to boom your wealth through the years.

Start your journey toward monetary freedom as early as viable. If you stay a lavish existence to your 20s, you'll become broke as quick as you hit your 40s. The great detail that you could do in your 20s is figuring out methods to multiply your wealth. If you manipulate to try this, you'll live lavishly for the relaxation of your life. So, the selection is yours.

Many humans in the US are searching for out methods to earn some more money. Gone are the instances on the same time as people have been satisfied with dwelling from paycheck to paycheck. Now, they need more. They need to get rid of that boring 9-five project. With the arrival of on line businesses, opportunities are masses, and I want you to utilize that possibility and do some factor big.

The quality manner to recognize passive income is to pit it in opposition to energetic earnings.

Active Income vs Passive Income

Active earnings is incomes a superb amount of money thru changing it sluggish into coins. The time component is essential right here. This way which you receives a fee with the resource of the hour. A regular nine-five mission is a conventional instance of this.

You get a hard and fast rate for the hours you determine for in per week or month. This technique that you earn cash so long as you located inside the artwork.

On the other, passive income is timeless. It doesn't include "renting" some time to gets a commission. It is a model that fetches you a excellent amount of income with out your complete-time involvement.

Active earnings includes a idea popularly called "No-Work-No-Pay" no longer like passive earnings.

This is exactly why maximum human beings are so intrigued about passive profits nowadays. It is like growing a income model as a way to print notes for you even as you're at the beach sunbathing in conjunction with your own family and buddies. Lucrative, isn't it?

However, growing a a fulfillment income version does require a few effort on the initial levels. Not surely every body has a assets to hire out or pretty some capital to spend money on a present day-day business enterprise. The excellent element approximately passive earnings is its massive fashion of channels. Plus, you do now not want to be extremely-rich to create a coins cow.

As I said in advance, developing the jump forward income model may also additionally occasionally take years. But in case you are inclined to earn cash at the same time as you sleep, then the effort is truely worth all the sleepless nights. It's all about the Foundation. To quote Gordon B. Hinckley, "You cannot gather a superb constructing on a susceptible foundation." Likewise, to create your dream profits model, you'll need to do the difficult yards initially. Once you offer you with a sustainable model, cash can be the final detail you'll be involved approximately.

Scope of Passive Income inside the 21st Century

Passive income is similar to the holy grail of cutting-edge wealth creation. Part of it's far due to its adequate channels. It is like an all-you-can-consume buffet! Passive earnings techniques have existed for loads of years dating again to the Middle Ages. With the appearance of the internet, many possibilities have spread out, and plenty of lovers are searching for to discover more.

I definitely have already informed you approximately apartment income, this is in all likelihood the maximum conventional instance of a passive profits supply. Another everyday instance is earning interest out of your financial financial savings account, constant deposits or routine deposits. This is regularly known as "creating a dwelling from cash".

Another "incomes earnings from money" scheme is to invest in shares or mutual fee range. Most of the time, we usually will be predisposed to maintain our tough-earned cash in saving bills with hobby charges as low as 0.01%. What if I inform you that you could earn now not less than $a hundred each month with out breaking a good deal sweat? Don't be surprised. It's viable. Investing in the correct shares is your solution. The hobby earned from stocks and mutual price range is quite immoderate in comparison to hobby earned from regular deposits and routine deposits. However, the danger is better within the case of shares and mutual budget. But that has now not deterred human beings from making an investment in shares due to its extended-time period blessings. We will communicate investment opportunities and their advantages in some time within the e book.

Another commonplace passive profits go with the flow is growing Facebook and YouTube content material. This choice has skyrocketed within the past decade with the improved accessibility of the net round the world. Many humans were capable of create a notable amount of passive earnings thru uploading content material material on YouTube and Facebook. The capability of social media systems in disseminating understanding and leisure to the hundreds has enabled many content material cloth creators to make a fortune.

I will refrain from imparting you with records that you already understand. Rental profits, stock investments and growing social media content material material is nothing new. You possibly recognize those channels of passive earnings. But do you realize the perfect strategies to discover those channels? My objective right right right here is that will help you well discover the ones channels. I will assist you discover some of the lesser-recognized channels of passive profits with big capability income. Once you're privy to the fundamentals of every passive profits source, you'll be financially independent and that could be my achievement.

Nowadays, we see an entire lot of startups bursting into the mainstream with revolutionary services and products. A lot of freshmen and professionals are taking the path of entrepreneurship to create a version that would help boom their coins exponentially. You ought to apprehend the vital distinction among a expert and an entrepreneur. A professional is someone who earns lively profits through supplying a positive company based mostly on his know-how. On the opportunity hand, an entrepreneur places all his efforts into growing a device which can assist him or her earn coins with out installing any attempt within the future.

Let me percentage with you an anecdote to help supply an cause of the difference among a expert and an entrepreneur. Water changed into scarce in a city. One of the townspeople Jim noticed in it an possibility to earn some income. So, every day he took buckets of water from the close by lake and allotted them some of the city parents in trade for some cash. He did this each day and the human beings of the metropolis paid him a few cash for his exploits. On the other hand, Will moreover perceived that he also can need to generate a few cash from this opportunity. So, he determined to create a pipeline some of the nearest lake to the metropolis and created a faucet water tool so that the townspeople ought to get as many buckets of water they need at a few level within the day. In the primary situation, Jim controlled to discover an possibility to earn some cash and decided to art work tough every day for it. However, Will did the smart element and created a sustainable version that would earn him coins for the relaxation of his lifestyles without operating tough every day. Not simplest that, in the future, he may additionally connect pipelines to close with the aid of the usage of cities to distribute water and boom his earnings exponentially. As really obvious, Jim become a expert who determined directly to art work difficult each day to earn an active earnings. Will created a recurrent sales version that helped him earn passive income in the course of his life without breaking a sweat. This is the crucial difference between a expert and an entrepreneur. However, an entrepreneur continuously has to suppose on his ft. This is because of the reality there can be a whole lot of opposition in the market whose version is probably greater useful to the overall public. That is why a positive entrepreneur has to design a version that isn't always simplest competitive however moreover sustainable. You must maintain one trouble in mind. Competitive Advantage has a constrained lifespan but in case you gain sustainable advantage out of your competition, you may relaxation confident that money will preserve screaming into your account.

Chapter 13: Channel #1 Facebook Content Cloth Material Creation

Content creation on social media web web sites, particularly on Facebook, is considered to be a superb supply of passive income in recent times. Facebook is one of the most importantly used applications in the international with an expected 2.7 billion active clients global.

More people are beginning to upload content material fabric cloth on Facebook because of its attain and recognition. If subjects are finished proper, you can earn anywhere among $500-$one thousand in keeping with day with out plenty trouble.

However, the task is to supply content material that sticks out from the organization. Around 500 million Facebook clients watch infinite motion pix every day. Your video have to be sincerely worth their attention. Wait a minute! That's no longer the real problem right here. The primary purpose of problem is that your movies may also acquire handiest 2% of your target market on Facebook. To growth your benefit, you want to understand how the Facebook set of rules works.

The Facebook Algorithm

Every time you turn on Facebook, its set of suggestions follows a 4-step approach to decide what should appear to your feed.

Step 1: Inventory

This set of policies inspects all the extremely-current statuses uploaded thru a client's friends and the pages they comply with.

Step 2: Signals

This is an set of regulations based totally on a customer's beyond behavior. It examines indicators like who uploaded the post, time spent on a median, engagement after importing content material fabric, feedback and tags, the diploma of information shared and so forth.

Step three: Predictions

This algorithm tries to assume how a specific patron will react to a selected publish. It predicts how possibly a effective purchaser can also remark, share, study or neglect approximately a wonderful submit.

Step 4: Score

This very last set of suggestions gadgets a relevance score for a positive positioned up after studying the various alerts and predictions of the user.

Remember: While arranging someone's feed, Facebook best considers the submit with the very high-quality relevance ratings.

How to earn cash from Facebook?

Now which you apprehend how the Facebook set of regulations works, allow me offer an cause for a way you can monetize your account.

There are many channels via which you may earn cash from Facebook. Each channel has its non-public set of eligibility requirements. Let me take you thru every channel in element.

1.   Including classified ads in Video:

You can also have seen commercials pop up from time to time while searching a Facebook video. That is how content fabric creators on Facebook make coins. Creators earn quite a few income from the advertisements that function on their movies.

There are 3 forms of in-circulate commercials that might be positioned on your movement pix. They are:

•   Pre-roll advertisements: These advertisements show up at the begin of movies.

•	Mid-roll advertisements: These commercials show up at herbal damage elements of movement pix

•	Image advertisements: These are static classified ads that function underneath content material.

There are first-rate eligibility requirements that must be met that permits you to feature in-flow into commercials to your movies like:

•	Content should be uploaded from an internet page and now not a profile.

•	You must abide thru Facebook's Partner Monetization pointers

•	Video publishing net page need to have at the least 10,000 enthusiasts.

•	Video duration need to be at the least 1 minute extended

- Your movies should pass the threshold of six hundred,000 mins of watch time inside the last 60 days.

- Video publishing net web page have to consist of at least five movies.

Meeting the above requirements coupled with a constant influx of lovers can fetch you a income of round $25,000-$30,000 every month. Fair deal, isn't it?

2. Fan Subscriptions:

Fan Subscriptions are advantages reserved for the committed lovers of your web web page. Your subscribers want to pay a few amount each month to have one-of-a-type get right of access to to your content cloth. You may additionally customize the advantages to be furnished in your subscribers in the form of personal interactions, merchandise benefits and so on.

The percentage of your profits generated from fan subscriptions is depending on the quantity contributed with the beneficial resource of your supporters. In case of internet transactions, you can gather the only hundred% of the price after taxes and costs. For cellular transactions (via Google or Apple), you may get hold of 70% of the fee because the cell issuer will maintain 30% of the charge for in-app purchases.

3.   Earning Money thru branded content material cloth cloth

This is a few other famous way to earn a exceptional deal of cash from Facebook. The magic tool is: Marry the brand your clients like with the emblem itself. Simply positioned, branded content material fabric fabric is a form of emblem collaboration in that you earn cash through promoting a fantastic brand for your web internet page/positioned up.

There are masses of producers on Facebook which might be eager to obtain out to tens of tens of millions of people. They might be inclined to pay you to promote their logo. Brands are well privy to the fact that human beings normally generally tend to bear in mind branded content cloth in choice to conventional advertising. This is due to the emotional charge your subscribers percentage with you. They are more likely to take note of the emblem you are endorsing in region of looking a industrial on Television.

Branded content is a huge step towards growing a modern day income skip as it's miles a win-win for every the content fabric cloth creators and the producers. Once your internet net web page is well-known, you could technique the producers for collaboration and earn a honest quantity of earnings via manner of endorsing them to your video/s.

4.   Earning cash from Live Video

Facebook has been a boon to many content material cloth creators. It has advanced from a informal chatting net site on line to a capability cash-making medium for tens of thousands and thousands. They did it with a few revolutionary inclusions down the street. The Facebook Stars is one such inclusion. With Facebook Stars, the traffic who music into your live video can show their help via buying and sending you the Stars.

There isn't always any cap to how a whole lot a certain viewer pays. One Facebook Star is really worth one cent. Cool, isn't it? Your traffic can definitely tap the Star icon subsequent to comments and make contributions the amount of their desire. If a person sends you 10,000 stars, you earn a complete of $a hundred. There are lots of video game streamers who earn hundreds of profits by using manner of using streaming video video games and interacting with their lovers. To get started, you really want to allow Stars and set up. Next factor, you'd be incomes a incredible deal of passive profits through the use of really interacting collectively in conjunction with your fans on Facebook.

How to Popularize your Facebook net internet web page

This is likely the maximum difficult bit. There are thousands and thousands of pages available. What are you able to do to face out from the institution? Why want to humans comply with you? First of all, you want to be prepared to simply accept the reality that getting to the ten,000 subscribers mark isn't any cakewalk. It takes months of cautious making plans and engagement. Remember, you are attempting to assemble a profits model just like a begin-up commercial enterprise agency. The war is real. The notable way to move approximately it is to be affected character and try hitting the number one a hundred subscribers mark, observed thru way of 500, then a thousand and so on. Rome modified into now not built in a day and your Facebook page gained't be both. Having said that, there are tactics to popularize your net page in a regular manner. I would possibly urge you to examine the steps I offer proper here so you can gain a incredible extensive form of followers at a normal tempo. Let's see how..

1. Invite Friends and Peers to Like and Share your internet page

As a number one step, you may invite your Facebook buddies and peers to love and percent your web page. This is the primary components that gives your page the preliminary throttle it goals. You can in reality go to the "Community" net web page and invite your buddies to like and percentage.

2. Post Original Content

Now that you have the guide of your near friends and pals, attention on posting actual content material fabric that keeps your subscribers engaged. How are you capable of do that?

•   Be proactive and conduct polls and placed up infographic content material

•   Provide informative statistics of coupons, suggests and masses of others.

•   Share backstage movies

three. Communicate with one-of-a-type Facebook pages

This is possibly the most surefire way to increase your fan base. You gets determined while you start interacting with unique clients. Share conversations and satisfactory chats with unique page connections. This will assist you win subscribers from specific pages.

four. Make Page Like advertisements

Creating an ad internet web web page will help you reach out to folks that aren't to your listing. This will help you rope in subscribers who is probably interested in your movement snap shots. This will help you increase your enthusiasts proper away.

5. Upload content fabric cloth at the same time as your lovers are active

We often make the error of timing our uploads. Do no longer truly upload your content material on every occasion you experience discover it not possible to face up to. As I already stated in advance, Facebook's set of guidelines may be unforgiving and so it's miles better to feature films at a time whilst maximum of your fanatics are energetic on Facebook. This will make certain that your fans get to appearance your films as quickly as you upload them. You want to investigate a piece. Check "Facebook Insights" and phrase which publish garnered the maximum engagement. Note the time of the video uploaded. Examine the fashion for approximately every week or , and you'll have a higher idea about at the identical time as to publish your movies to make certain most crowd engagement.

6. Resort to Unconventional advertising

Unconventional advertising remains pretty super. There are many motives why. Let me allude to Red Bull's genius tactic in this regard. In the childhood of Red Bull, organization officers determined to place empty cans in trash packing containers outside famous pubs frequented with the aid of more youthful human beings. This made the emblem appear famous to the youngsters. Within no time, the emblem have become a darling to the younger population- their key purpose phase. This is also known as Guerilla Marketing. My component right right here is the more locations your Facebook web page advertisements seem, the more reputation it will benefit. So, located your Facebook web page hyperlink to key regions like your electronic mail signature, internet net page footer, blog, exclusive social media pages. Following this tactic will growth your chances of getting noticed.

Once you are capable of get keep of a huge kind of fans on your internet web page, many doorways of passive income possibilities can be opened for you. If you've got a study the techniques mentioned in this ebook, followers will begin multiplying very quickly. There may be some impediments on the way within the form of gradual increase or an unfortunate droop however that want to not deter you from popularizing your account. As I already stated in advance than, it's all in the Foundation.

Chapter 14: Channel #2: Apps And Websites Review

The Internet has changed the lives of such pretty a few. In this aspect in time, nearly some aspect is feasible with the Internet. It is a blessing. Just visit an app or internet site, pick out out objects of your choice and feature them brought to your doorstep right away. Why exit whilst you can actually rub your magic lamp (phone) and get subjects introduced in your cope with? There are severa apps and web web sites to be had which is probably flocked with the resource of thousands and heaps of humans which encompass you and me each day to order products of our liking. Apps and Websites are large time savers. No! Not without a doubt that. They are passive cash makers too.

The international of the Internet is evaluation pushed. It isn't always possible for clients to gauge the exceptional of products on a virtual net internet web page or app. This is wherein reviews are available accessible. Customers can actually test the critiques left thru way of various clients who used the product to decide on whether or now not or not they should buy the product. Online evaluations not most effective assist customers pick the right product but additionally lets in organizations curate the terrific products for his or her customers.

Many corporations who have products included up in apps and websites hire humans to attempt out products and evaluate them simply so their customers have to make an informed choice in advance than trying to find a positive product. As there is lots of competition to be had, maximum companies try to painting a purchaser-centric technique to rope in and maintain clients. This is why they hire app and internet website reviewers to increase website visitors and provide the clients a healthful revel in.

Why Companies pay for reviews?

You can earn a giant amount of passive profits by using manner of reviewing apps and internet web sites. Companies can be willing to pay you for reviewing their apps for the subsequent motives:

1. To boom Traffic:

Customer evaluations pressure site visitors to apps and web web sites. If you are seeking out "exceptional inns near me" on Google, you will see a list of lodges with excellent rankings. One resort can also additionally have a score of three.Five. Another may additionally furthermore have a rating of 4.Five. Which one will you select? The one with the higher rating, right? Reviews and rankings help clients pick out the proper alternative. Reviews and rankings make web sites and apps appealing to customers resulting in advanced website online traffic.

2. To decorate search engine optimization

A examine located that ninety% of clients study critiques online earlier than going to a web (or offline) business corporation). Eighty four% of them take into account online reviews as an entire lot as they take delivery of as real with word-of-mouth pointers. Ninety three % of customers do not forget that their shopping for alternatives are motivated via evaluations before they click on on the "Buy Now" button.

Now, for Google, the customer comes first. If an app or internet site has fantastic evaluations from clients, Google will rank it better than others. The opportunities of the app's visibility to extraordinary customers additionally will increase. Not most effective that, splendid critiques from clients also seem the truth that the app or internet internet web page is simple. All in all, with high-quality critiques, an app or net web site can be in Google's appropriate books.

3. To decorate Sales

In earnings, the client is God. A brand's popularity is relying on the feedback of its customers. Online evaluations have an impact on clients to move for a high pleasant emblem or product, thereby growing income. A proper assessment of a certain product guarantees an increase in profits.

four. The Trust Factor

A a fulfillment business garners sustainable benefit from its competition. Nowadays, maximum humans maintain on-line and they can't choose the outstanding of the goods on a digital product. That is why they do not forget purchaser reviews. An honest assessment of a high quality product can growth the credibility of a high high-quality app or web page. Once you construct that accept as true with with the client, she or he may be able to start endorsing your organisation.

Now, I preference that I had been capable of stress the importance of on-line app reviews in using profits. As an increasing number of groups turn out to be determined to pressure in customers, you could earn a handsome amount of passive income through manner of reviewing gadgets for the ones companies.

You can earn everywhere among $4 hundred-$800 each month via way of writing opinions on merchandise for a wonderful organisation. Follow those guidelines to ensure that your evaluations stand proud of the rest:

• Start thru the usage of trying the product out and have a look at its competencies

• Focus at the target audience and count on from their attitude

• Provide an in-intensity and high-quality assessment of the product

- Provide salient competencies of the product and its after-income company

- Your evaluation must be honest. Mention the horrific features of the product as nicely.

- Use instances from your usage of the product

- Always try and price the product

- Keep it crisp and precise

- Proofread your evaluation to test for grammatical errors or use of excessive jargon

Popular Websites that pay for on line reviews

There are lots of internet net websites to be had that pay for writing on-line critiques. Some of the maximum famous net internet web sites are:

1. ReviewStream

This is a net web web page that may pay you for writing evaluations on any product on its platform. Pen down a assessment for a product which you have used, and you can receives a commission.

This net internet page moreover gives a cash bonus for reviews that get approval (inside the shape of votes) from other individuals. Remember, your remarks need to be exquisite and consistent with the internet net page's publishing pointers. Payment is probably made to your PayPal account.

2. Software Judge:

This net site will pay you for writing critiques on Software. They can pay you around $50 for positive reviews, and you could post a most of three reviews steady with day. Explore their internet site for unlimited passive profits possibilities.

3. Gen Video

This net site makes a speciality of generating video opinions for the customers. If you have particular communication competencies, then you could sell positive merchandise thru YouTube movies and earn a significate amount of associate income.

four. Slice the Pie

This is a song compare app which can pay the reviewers for leaving a compare after being attentive to a track. Interesting, isn't it? You can clearly visit the internet web page, pay attention to a modern song for as a minimum 90 seconds and pen down your evaluation. A focused examine can fetch you a huge quantity of income.

Milton Keynes UK
Ingram Content Group UK Ltd.
UKHW032324121024
449589UK00010B/371

9 781998 927258